IN NO TIME

Windows
98

IN NO TIME

Windows 98

Günter Born

Prentice Hall Europe

London New York Toronto Sydney Tokyo Singapore Madrid Mexico City Munich Paris

First published in 1998 as Easy - Windows 98 by
Markt&Technik Buch - und Software Verlag GmbH
85540 Haar bei München/Germany
This edition published 1999 by
Prentice Hall Europe
Campus 400, Maylands Avenue
Hemel Hempstead
Hertfordshire, HP2 7EZ

A division of
Simon & Schuster International Group

Translated by Berlitz Translation Services UK, Baldock, Hertfordshire

Typeset in Stone Sans
by Berlitz Translation Services UK, Desktop Publishing Department

Designed and Produced by Berlitz Translation Services UK, Desktop Publishing Department

Printed and bound in Great Britain
by MPG Books Ltd, Bodmin, Cornwall

Library of Congress Cataloging-in-Publication Data
Available from the publisher
British Library Cataloguing in Publication Data
A catalogue record for this book is available from the British Library
ISBN 0-13-977679-6

1 2 3 4 5 03 02 01 00 99

Contents

2 Working with programs 50

3 Managing files and folders 64

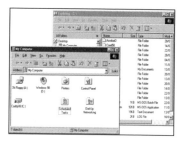

4 Writing and drawing in Windows — 134

8 Internet and Web Surfing with Windows — 262

9 Networking with Windows 298

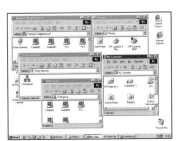

Dear Readers,

This book has been written to guide you through your first steps with Windows 98. If you can share my belief that working with Windows is actually quite easy and can even be fun, you will acquire step by step the basic knowledge for working with Windows-based computers. Read the first three chapters to learn about using the mouse, windows and programs, to find out what files and folders are used for and how to insert a diskette into a floppy disk drive. Step by step illustrated instructions will show you how.

In the remaining chapters, you will learn all the things you can do with Windows. After just a few steps you will be able to write your first letter and format an invitation. How about using the computer to listen to music CDs, watch videos or relax with a game? Would you like to know what "surfing the Internet" involves? Maybe you haven't got access to the Internet yet? No matter — this course will give you a taste of the technology. But read for yourself what Windows can do.

Oh, just a final point: take your time and relax. A lot is learnt through repetition, almost incidentally. So have fun with Windows and with this book.

Günter Born

The following three pages show you how the computer keyboard is constructed. Groups of keys are dealt with individually to make it easier to understand. A majority of the computer keys operate in the same way as on a typewriter. However, there are also some additional keys which are designed for the peculiarities of computer work. See for yourself . . .

Typewriter keys

You use these keys exactly as you do on a typewriter.
You also use the Enter key to send commands to the computer

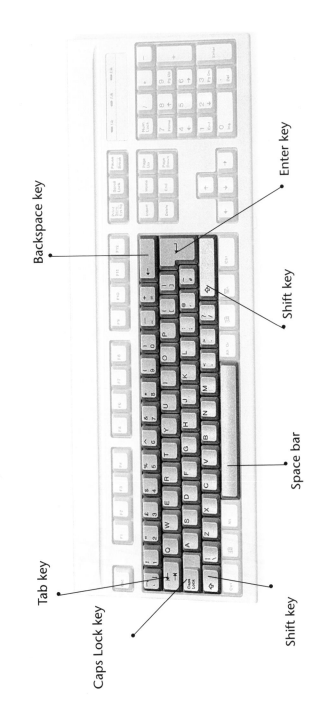

Backspace key

Enter key

Shift key

Tab key

Caps Lock key

Space bar

Shift key

Special keys, function keys, numeric keypad, status lights

Special keys and function keys are used for particular tasks in computer operation; Ctrl, Alt and Alt Gr keys are mostly used in combination with other keys. The Esc key can be used to cancel commands, and Insert and Delete can be used, amongst other things, to insert and delete text.

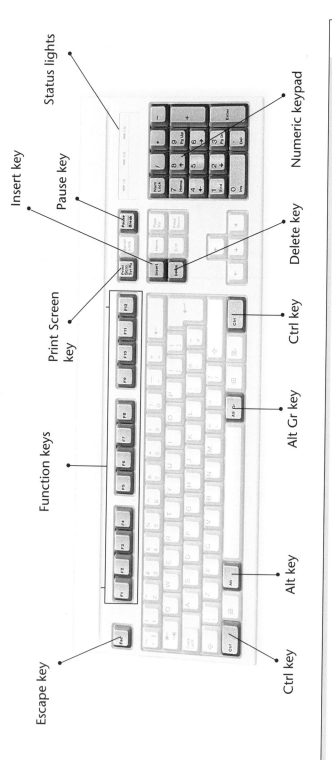

Status lights

Numeric keypad

Insert key

Pause key

Delete key

Print Screen key

Ctrl key

Function keys

Alt Gr key

Escape key

Alt key

Ctrl key

Navigational keys

These keys are used to move around the screen.

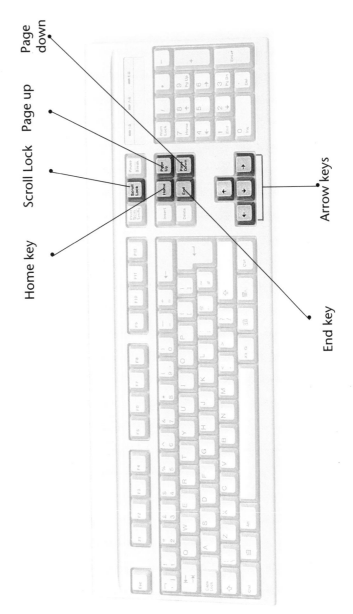

Page down

Page up

Scroll Lock

Home key

Arrow keys

End key

"Click (on) ..."
means: press once
briefly on the button.

Clicking with the
left-hand mouse
button

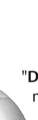

Clicking with the
right-hand mouse
button

"Double-click (on) ..."
means: press the left-
hand button briefly
twice in quick
succession.

Double-clicking

"Drag ..."
means: click on an object with the left-hand
mouse button, keep the button pressed,
move the mouse and thus drag the item to
another position.

Dragging

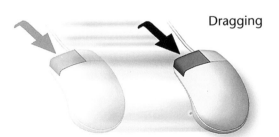

1

Basics and first steps

What's in this chapter?

In this chapter you will learn the basics of working with Windows 98. After reading it you will be able to start and close Windows. You will also get to know the most important elements of the Windows screen. You will be able to work with the mouse and will know what pointing, dragging, clicking and double-clicking are. In addition, you will know how to work with windows: how windows can be opened, closed, moved and resized. You will also know how to get information using Windows Help.

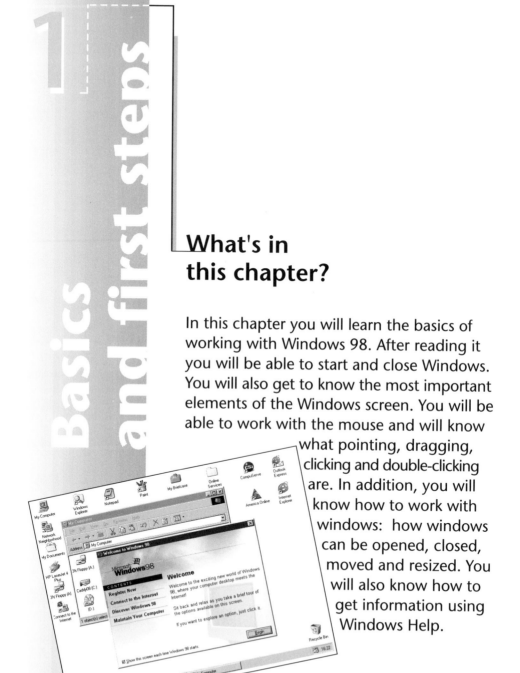

You are going to learn about:

Starting Windows

Before you can work with Windows 98 you have to switch on the computer and start up Windows.

1 Switch on the computer and monitor.

Windows takes a few seconds to load.

In a **network** Windows shows this logon dialog box (see also Chapter 11).

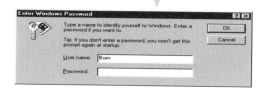

2 Press the Esc key to bypass the logon.

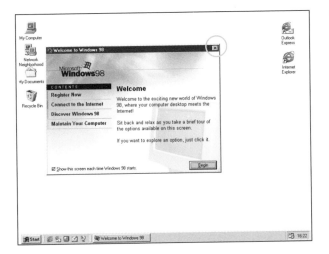

This picture appears as soon as Windows is loaded. Look at the window *Welcome to Windows 98?* Now try to close it. (Unfortunately at this point we must move on, but you will find out more about this window later on in this chapter.)

3 Move the mouse until the little arrow points to the top right corner of the window.

4 Now press the left mouse button.

Windows will now close the *Welcome to Windows 98* window.

Is your screen still dark? Perhaps you forgot to switch on the monitor. Also check whether all cables are connected and the plug is in the socket. Likewise for the computer if nothing happens after switching on.

21

A desktop - what is it?

As soon as you have logged on, Windows presents a picture similar to that shown below.

This is the Windows working area (or the **user interface**) known as the **desktop**. Just like working at a desk, you will find various office tools (computer, waste-paper basket etc.) which you frequently work with.

By **user interface** we mean the way the computer accepts information from the user and displays information. Windows has, for example, a graphical interface with icons and windows.

Maybe your desktop has more icons, windows, a green background or even a picture? This isn't really a problem. Each user can adjust Windows to suit his or her requirements; also on installing programs the desktop often changes. The picture above shows only selected desktop elements. You will learn about other elements and their functions in the various chapters of this book.

The **My Computer** icon contains all the functions (these are also called **resources**) for working with files like letters, pictures etc. and programs on your computer. You will learn more about this in the following chapters.

Can you see the **Network Neighborhood** icon on your desktop? This means your computer is linked by a cable to other computers in a network and you can use this icon to access functions for exchanging data with other computers on a network (see Chapter 9).

Network Neighborhood

If there is something (for example a letter) you no longer need, then simply "move" this document into the Recycle Bin. Exactly how this works you will find out in Chapter 3.

Recycle Bin

The grey bar at the bottom border of the screen is called the **taskbar**.

In this bar Windows displays various items of information.

On the right of the taskbar Windows shows the **time**.

The Start **button** in the left hand corner of the taskbar is used, for example, to call up (activate) programs.

These little icons also represent buttons. They are used to directly activate certain programs or functions.

WHAT'S THIS?

Buttons are rectangular elements that are often used in Windows for activating particular functions (this is like in a cassette recorder where you can press switches for play, fast forward and rewind).

You will get to know the other functions on the taskbar in the following pages and in Chapter 2.

Working with the mouse

The **mouse** is so-called because it bears some resemblance to a real mouse. Most of them have two **buttons** (sometimes even three). The mouse can be moved over the desktop and you can press the mouse buttons.

We often refer to pressing a mouse button as **clicking**. You have already met this at the beginning of the chapter when closing the *Welcome to Windows 98* window. For Windows you need only the left and right mouse buttons. If your mouse has a middle button, it will usually be controlled by an auxiliary program that belongs to the mouse and is described in the relevant handbook. You will learn how to work with the mouse and operate the left and right mouse buttons in the following pages.

Put your hand on the mouse with the index finger on the left button and the middle finger on the right button. The mouse should also be placed on a rubber or foam mat (called a **mouse mat**). These mats are more suitable than a smooth table top for working with the mouse.

1 Put your hand on the mouse.

2 Move the mouse about on the mat. You do not need to press any button while doing this. You will see a little arrow on the desktop.

As soon as you move the mouse, the arrow moves with it on the screen. This little arrow is also called **a mouse pointer** (and also sometimes, incorrectly, a **mouse cursor**).

3 Move the mouse until the mouse pointer points to the *My Computer* icon. This is referred to as **pointing** with the mouse. You can use the mouse to point to all the desktop elements (i.e. the Recycle Bin, taskbar etc.).

Actually it's not quite correct to speak of "**pointing the mouse**". The mouse in fact remains on your desk and you use the mouse pointer to point to a screen element. However this term is in general use and will therefore also be adopted in this book.

4 Now **point** with the **mouse** to the Start button in the **taskbar**.

When pointing to some elements, a little text window appears called a **text label**. In a text label Windows gives you additional information.

5 Now **point** the **mouse** to the **time** in the bottom right hand corner of the window.

25

Windows opens the text label window and brings up the **day of the week** and the **date**. As soon as you take the mouse away from this element, Windows automatically closes the text label window.

Pointing with the mouse is really quite simple, isn't it? Besides pointing, the mouse has another function which is called **clicking**. This is quite easy too:

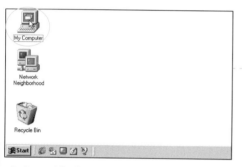

1 Point with the mouse to the *My Computer* icon.

2 Now press the left mouse button and then release it again. This is called **clicking**.

The icon you have just clicked will now be highlighted in colour. Highlighting an element in this way with a mouse click is also called **selecting**.

3 Click with the mouse on a free area of the desktop.

Windows cancels the coloured selection of the icon leaving only the icon name in a broken frame. This frame indicates which icon was last selected.

4 Now try and click with the left mouse button on the Start button. A little window opens: it is called the **start menu**.

5 Click on any free area of the desktop to reclose the start menu.

You will frequently meet the term **menu** in Windows. A menu is a small window containing various names. As with a menu in a restaurant, you can also choose an item in Windows from a menu by clicking with the mouse. Via the **start menu** you can activate programs or other Windows functions (see Chapter 2).

Besides pointing and clicking, you can also **drag** (things) with the mouse:

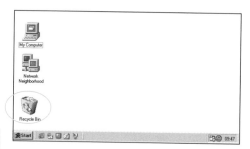

1 Point to the Recycle Bin icon with the mouse pointer.

2 Press the left mouse button but this time keep it pressed and now drag the Recycle Bin icon across the screen. A second Recycle Bin icon is displayed which moves with the mouse pointer.

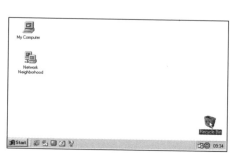

3 Once you have dragged the Recycle Bin icon into the right-hand corner of the desktop, let go of the left mouse button. Windows will now move the Recycle Bin icon to the spot where you released the left mouse button.

After dragging an icon or window, it will still be selected. To deselect an icon after dragging, click any free area on the desktop with the mouse.

The last important function you can carry out with the mouse is called **double-clicking**. By double-clicking, windows can be opened and programs started.

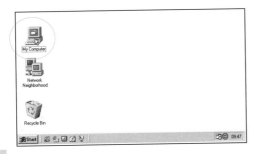

1 Point to the *My Computer* icon.

2 Briefly press the left mouse button twice in succession. It is important that these clicks follow each other in quick succession.

If everything goes well, Windows will now open this window with the name *My Computer*.

The content of the window depends on the particular icon chosen each time you double click. Don't worry if your icons are displayed smaller or if the buttons at the top of the window contain text. All this can be adjusted under Windows.

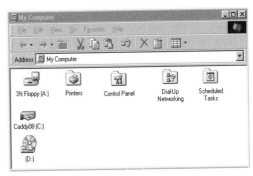

Working with windows

Windows executes programs and functions in windows which display information. To quickly find your way around, you should know the most important elements of a window. In addition, you must also know how to open, resize and close a window.

1 Open the *My Computer* window by double clicking on its icon.

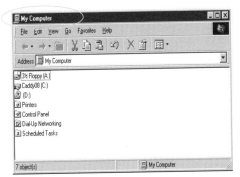

The structure of all windows is largely the same. The *My Computer* window is therefore typical.

At the top of the window you will find what is called the **title bar** where Windows displays the name of the window.

Beneath the title bar you will see that many windows have a **menu bar** with names like FILE, EDIT, VIEW etc. You can use these menus to call up the associated functions.

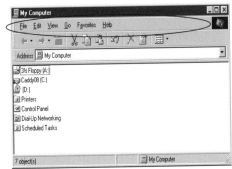

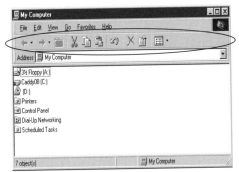

Many windows also have a **toolbar** which you can often use to call up functions directly without having to take a slower path via menus.

Along the bottom border, many windows also have a **status bar** for displaying additional information. In the status bar shown here, Windows indicates that the window contains 15 icons (also called **objects**). In addition you will see that it is the contents of *My Computer* which are being displayed.

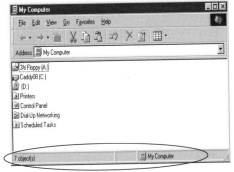

31

For your first steps you will only need the icons of the three little buttons on the right in the title bar. Using these buttons, a window can be closed or resized. Most windows have at least one or two of these buttons.

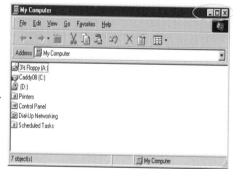

2 As an experiment point to the middle button in the opened window *My Computer*. As soon as you point to the button Windows brings up a note about its function in a text label window.

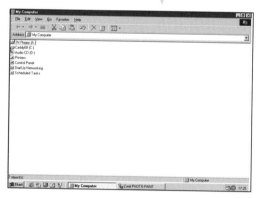

3 Now click on the middle button.

Windows expands the window to fill the entire screen. We say that the window has been **maximized**. Observe that the icon for the middle button has changed.

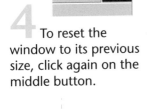

4 To reset the window to its previous size, click again on the middle button.

5 Now click once in the top right corner of the window on the left button ▬.

The window disappears from the desktop. However, if you look closely, it has only shrunk to an icon. You will find the icon as a button in the taskbar.

6 To open the window, click on the *My Computer* button in the taskbar.

33

Now it only remains to shut down an open window.

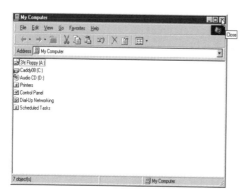

Click in the top right corner of the window on the button ☒.

This button will completely shut down the window. You will recognize this by the fact that the icon disappears from the taskbar.

Changing the window size

In the previous step you used the buttons in the top right corner to expand a window to the full size of the screen or to shrink it to an icon. However, it is often better to gradually adjust a window to the desired size. This is very simple to do in Windows.

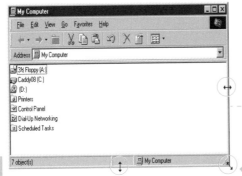

1 Now try this out by pointing with the mouse to the right border of a window.

2 Point to the bottom border and to one of the corners.

As soon as you point to the correct place at the edge of the window, the mouse pointer assumes the form of a double-headed arrow. You might need to move the mouse around a little until this appears. The double-headed arrow indicates the direction in which the window size can be changed. You can therefore use the left/right edge of the window to alter its width. The top/bottom edge of the window alters the height and by using the corners the size of the window can be adjusted whilst keeping the proportions the same.

3 Point again to the border of the window.

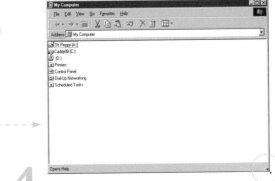

4 When the double-headed arrow appears, drag the border of the window in the desired direction whilst holding the left mouse button down.

35

Depending on the setup, Windows indicates the new window size as soon as you drag it or represents it by a broken line.

5 When the window reaches the desired size, release the left mouse button.

Windows will now adjust the size of the window accordingly.

Moving windows

One of the strengths of Windows lies in the fact that you can work with several programs or windows at once. Perhaps you would like to try this for yourself.

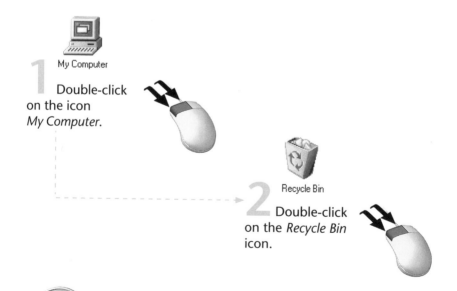

My Computer

1 Double-click on the icon *My Computer.*

Recycle Bin

2 Double-click on the *Recycle Bin* icon.

If you have carried out this step correctly, you will see two windows on the desktop. Unfortunately these two windows overlap and the content of the background window will be partly hidden.

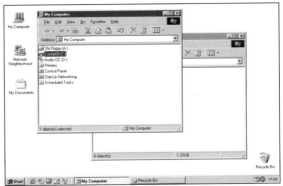

You could of course close a window; or click the mouse on the window in the background (or its button in the taskbar) in order to bring it into the foreground. However, you will often want to arrange the two windows side by side so as see the contents of both at the same time. This however is not quite so easy: dragging the border of the window will only change its size; and trying to drag the contents of the window will not work either. To move a window a little trick is therefore necessary.

Point the mouse at the **title bar** of the **window**.

Then **drag** the **window** using the mouse to the position you want.

Depending on the setting, Windows will move the window or indicate the new window position during the dragging operation by a broken line.

37

3 As soon as the window is at the position you want, release the left mouse button.

Windows will move the window to the new position. If the window sizes have been appropriately chosen you will now be able to see both windows on the desktop.

Scrolling the window

What happens if the content of the window is too large to fit the current size of window displayed?

1 Open the *My Computer* window.

2 Reduce the window until part of the content disappears.

Here you can see the *My Computer* window which has been appropriately reduced.

As soon as the window can no longer display all the information, the window acquires what is called a **scroll bar** on the right or bottom border. This scroll bar allows you to choose a different part of the window content for viewing. You can think of this as a kind of "scrolling".

To move the content in a window using the scroll bar, proceed as follows:

1 Point the mouse at the rectangular area within the scroll bar. This area is also called the **scroll box**.

2 Now drag the scroll box with the mouse in the desired direction. Windows then displays other sections of the window content.

Both the above pictures only show a horizontal scroll bar. Windows may also have a vertical scroll bar, in which case the window contents can be moved up or down. When writing a text, you can use this scroll bar to scroll through the text.

At the ends of the scroll bar you will see two buttons ◀ and ▶. If you find scrolling with the scroll box too awkward, you can scroll through the document in stages by clicking on the appropriate button with the mouse.

Getting help

After reading this book, you will probably still have some questions and maybe the Windows built-in Help function will answer these for you. To display the window for the Windows Help function, proceed as follows:

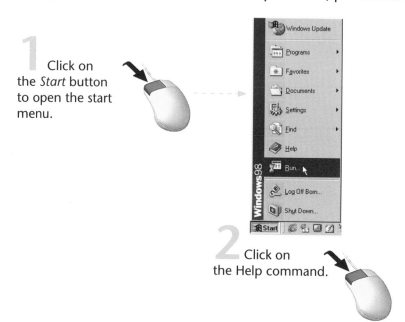

1 Click on the *Start* button to open the start menu.

2 Click on the Help command.

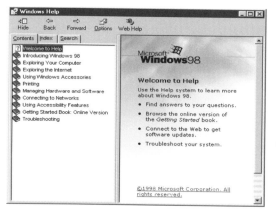

Windows will now open the two-part Help window. These parts are called frames. The left frame contains three **tabs** with the names *Content*, *Index* and *Search*. The right frame displays the Help text.

In many windows there is not enough room to display all the information. Windows therefore uses what are callled "index cards". The index cards are arranged one behind the other and each one can be brought into the foreground by clicking its tab. You then only see the contents of the top index card.

The *Contents* tab works like the index of a book. The individual headings are identified by stylized books or pages.

3 Double-click on a closed-book icon 📖 to see the list of subtopics.

4 Clicking with the mouse on the ? symbol opens the help page required.

The contents of the selected help page appear in the right frame. You can scroll through the text by using the scroll bar.

Underlined text represents a cross-reference (hyperlink) to other information. If you point to one of these hyperlinks, the mouse pointer takes the form of a hand. Clicking the mouse on the hyperlink displays the associated topic.

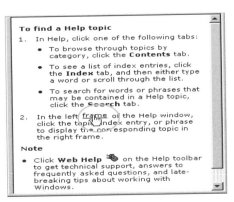

To find a Help topic

1. In Help, click one of the following tabs:

 • To browse through topics by category, click the **Contents** tab.

 • To see a list of index entries, click the **Index** tab, and then either type a word or scroll through the list.

 • To search for words or phrases that may be contained in a Help topic, click the **Search** tab.

2. In the left frame of the Help window, click the topic, index entry, or phrase to display the corresponding topic in the right frame.

Note

 • Click **Web Help** 🌐 on the Help toolbar to get technical support, answers to frequently asked questions, and late-breaking tips about working with Windows.

⇦ Back | ⇨ Forward

If you have clicked a hyperlink or activated several Help pages, you can switch between these pages using *Forward* and *Back*.

WHAT'S THIS?

Hyperlink is a term that often crops up in connection with Internet documents. A hyperlink defines a reference to a related document. As soon as you select this reference the related document will be displayed.

You can also search selectively in Help for particular terms. The *Index* tab corresponds to the index of a book.

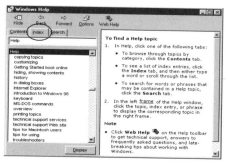

 Click the *Index* tab.

 Type the **search term** in the little box above the list of index entries.

If there is a matching keyword, Windows indicates this in the lower half of the window.

WHAT'S THIS?

You will meet this kind of input box with increasing frequency. They are also called **fields** or **text fields**.

Click on the found term in the list and then click *Display*.

The associated Help text now appears in the right frame of the Help window.

TIP

Long texts can be scrolled in the right-hand frame using the scroll bar. Are other windows hidden by the Help window? If so, reduce the size of the Help window or close it.

Windows Help also allows you to search for any particular term.

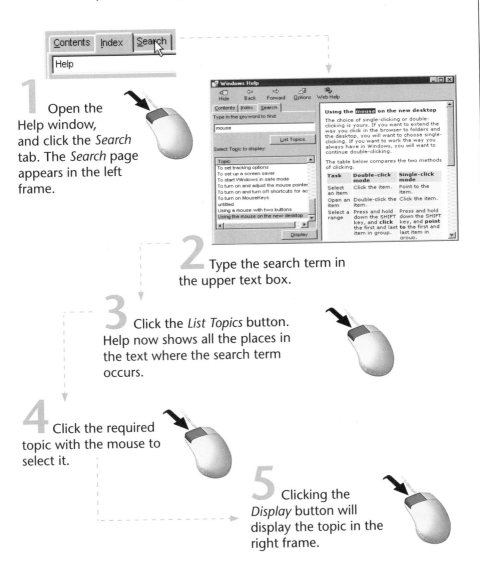

1 Open the Help window, and click the *Search* tab. The *Search* page appears in the left frame.

2 Type the search term in the upper text box.

3 Click the *List Topics* button. Help now shows all the places in the text where the search term occurs.

4 Click the required topic with the mouse to select it.

5 Clicking the *Display* button will display the topic in the right frame.

If there is no program
window open, you can
also activate Windows
Help directly by means
of the F1 key.

In addition, various programs support calling up the Help window. The
example shown here is for the *My Computer* window.

1 Open the *My
Computer* window.

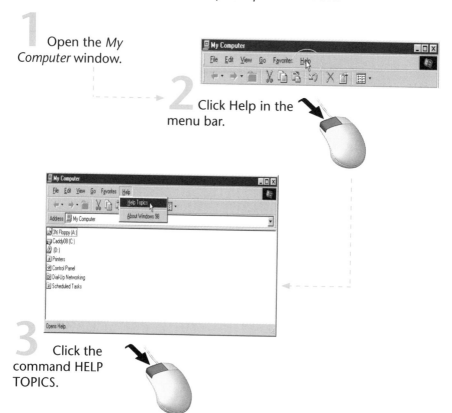

2 Click Help in the
menu bar.

3 Click the
command HELP
TOPICS.

Windows displays the window with the three tabs *Contents, Index* and
Search.

When pointing to different objects, do you find the text label displayed
by Windows helpful? The same sort of thing is provided in some
program windows.

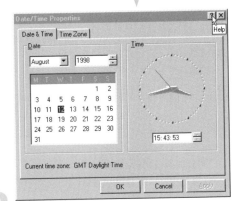

1 Double-click the time on the taskbar. Windows opens a window showing the calendar and time.

2 Click the *Help* button top right. The mouse pointer now looks like this .

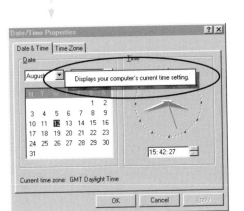

3 Click any element in the window (i.e. the year field). Windows will now display a direct help window with information on the element concerned.

To close the Help window, click anywhere else in the window.

45

The window for displaying the date and time is also called a **Properties dialog box**. Windows uses these dialog boxes to display the properties of an object (in this case the time and date) and to enable them to be changed by the user. Properties are always grouped on an index card.

On starting Windows, does the *Welcome to Windows 98* window appear? You can even get information on this.

1 Insert the Windows CD-ROM into the drive.

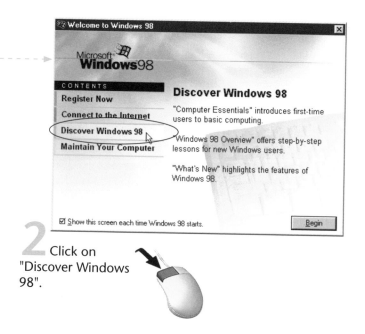

2 Click on "Discover Windows 98".

Windows now starts an interactive tutorial program in which you can call up various lessons on the operation of Windows. You only need to click on the topics you require to select the tutorial. You can end the program via the *Close* button.

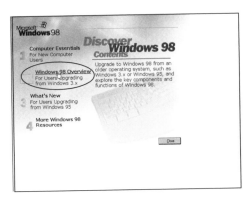

If you don't want to see the *Welcome to Windows 98* window on the next startup:

1 Click the **check box** "Show this screen on each start". The check mark (tick) in the check box should disappear.

2 Click the *Close* button in the top right corner of the window.

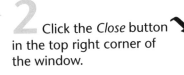

WHAT'S THIS?

The small rectangle in the bottom left corner is known as a check box; they occur in many windows and enable you to switch a particular option on or off. A check mark (a tick here, but a cross in some applications) indicates that the option is set. Clicking alternately sets and clears the check mark.

Shutting down Windows

Before taking the next steps, one question still remains: how is Windows actually shut down?

CAUTION

Never just switch the computer off to exit Windows. This may lead to data being lost and no longer being able to start Windows!

You might have thought about simply switching off the computer and the monitor. This would of course force Windows to shut down. After having shut down any loaded programs and closed any windows that may have been open, you must shut down Windows methodically.

1 Click the Start button in the taskbar. Windows opens the Start menu.

Windows Update

HP LaserJet 4 Plus

Programs ▶

Favorites ▶

Documents ▶

Settings ▶

Find ▶

Help

Run...

Log Off Tony...

Shut Down...

Start

2 Click in the Start menu on the command "Shut Down". Windows will now open the dialog box *Shut Down Windows*.

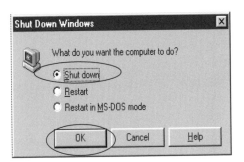

Click the shut down **option** followed by the *OK* button.

WHAT'S THIS?

In some windows, Windows waits for an input from the user; these windows are known as **dialog boxes**. In the *Shut Down Windows* dialog box shown in the example above, Windows waits for you to confirm shut down.

WHAT'S THIS?

Radio buttons are the small circles inside a dialog box. Click on one of these to select an option. The radio button with the dot marks the selected option. In contrast to **check boxes**, only one option can be selected within any group.

Windows recognizes the request to shut down and begins "cleaning up". This involves saving data on the hard disk, shutting down any programs that may be running and saving the settings for the next Windows start up.

It's now safe to turn off your computer.

As soon as this text appears on the screen you can switch off the computer.

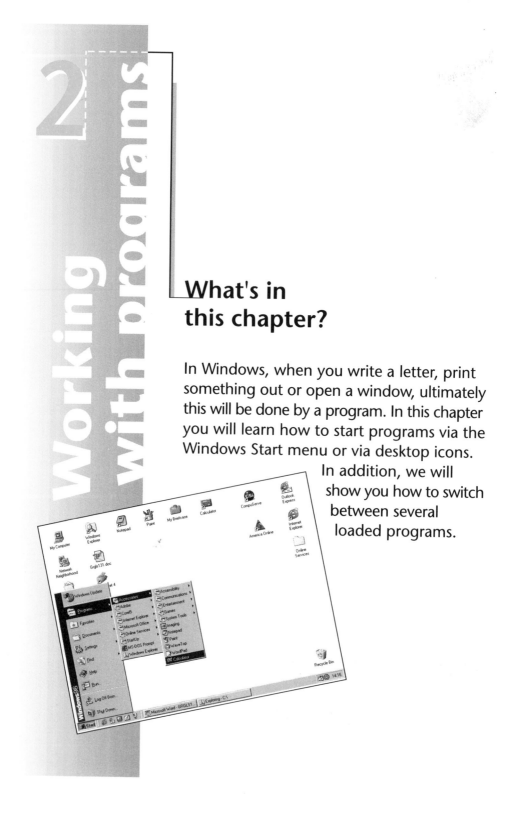

2

Working with programs

What's in
this chapter?

In Windows, when you write a letter, print
something out or open a window, ultimately
this will be done by a program. In this chapter
you will learn how to start programs via the
Windows Start menu or via desktop icons.
In addition, we will
show you how to switch
between several
loaded programs.

You already know about:

You are going to learn about:

The Start menu

You have already met the **Start menu** briefly in Chapter 1.

 Click the Start button
in the left lower corner of
the screen.

Windows opens a small window with various icons and names. This
window is called the **Start menu**. Similar to a menu in a restaurant, you
can choose from different items. These items are Windows commands
by means of which you can activate various functions, open submenus
or start programs. We have already done this in Chapter 1 to call up
Windows Help with the Help command.

Starting programs

You actually already know how to start a program. When working through Chapter 1 did you open the *My Computer* window by double-clicking the icon? Or did you call up Windows Help via the Start menu? What you were actually doing was starting programs. However, there are many more programs under Windows and many of these are activated via the **Start menu**. The routine is the same for different programs. So we shall illustrate starting a program by way of an example.

1 Open the Start menu with a single mouse click on the Start button.

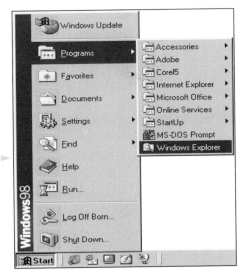

2 Click the item Programs in the Start menu. Windows opens a further window called a **submenu**.

There you will see the icons for programs such as Internet Explorer, Microsoft Word and Windows Explorer, depending on which programs have been installed on your computer.

3 Click on the item Windows Explorer in the submenu of the menu item Programs.

Windows then starts the program *Explorer*. The window for this opens on the desktop.

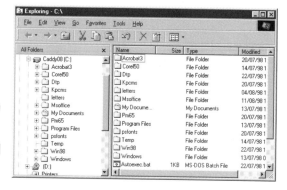

How to work with this program will be covered in Chapter 3.

In this way you can start all programs that are entered as icons in the Start menu.

Examples will be found in the following pages of this book.

In the previous step we activated a program directly in the submenu Programs. Many programs though are found elsewhere in the Start menu. Now we will activate the Calculator. The following steps are required for this.

Open the Start menu again by clicking on the Start button.

Then click the menu item Programs.

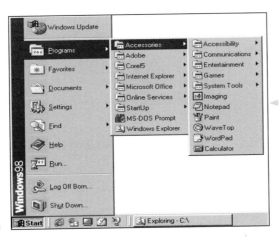

In the Programs submenu click the entry Accessories.

In the Accessories submenu click the entry Calculator.

55

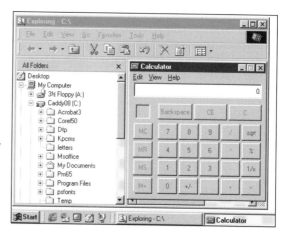

Now the Windows Calculator starts up as an additional program. If you did not close the window for Explorer it will probably be partially hidden by *Calculator*.

Besides entries for programs, the Start menu contains other menu items with the icon . This icon (and the small triangle at the right edge of an item) indicate **program groups** (e.g. STARTUP, ACCESSORIES etc.). Program groups bring several program icons (or other groups) together into a **submenu**. Clicking the icon of a program group opens a further **submenu** which may show icons for further program groups or programs. In the program group ACCESSORIES you will, for example, find further subgroups such as ENTERTAINMENT or SYSTEM TOOLS. Which menus and submenus you see in the Start menu will depend on the programs installed.

Switching programs

Windows enables you to have several programs loaded at the same time. You can then switch between the different programs and even exchange data between them.

1 Open the Start menu and click Programs/Accessories.

Imaging
Notepad
Paint

2 Click the entry Notepad in the Accessories menu.

From the previous steps, the desktop now has three overlapping windows belonging to the programs you have started. You can now work with the calculator, write a letter or look at files without having to first shut down the most recently used program.

Exploring - C:\   Calculator   Untitled - Notepad

3 For example, to work with the calculator, click on its icon in the taskbar.

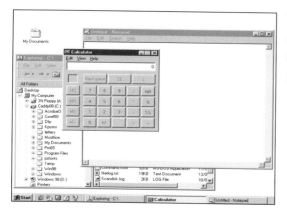

The calculator window now comes to the foreground and you can work with the program.

In the **taskbar**, Windows displays the **icons** of loaded **programs**; the button of the active window will be shown "depressed". It is possible to **change** to another **program window** at any time by clicking the relevant **button** in the taskbar.

In addition to the buttons on the taskbar, you can also use the key combination ⟨Alt⟩+⟨⇄⟩ to toggle (switch) between programs. Hold the ⟨Alt⟩ key down and press the ⟨⇄⟩ key.

Windows displays a window with the icons of the loaded programs, as in this example. Each time the ⟨⇄⟩ key is pressed another program is selected. On releasing the ⟨Alt⟩ key, the most recently selected program window is brought into the foreground.

Exiting programs

You have already learned the methods for closing a window in Chapter 1. You can exit a program in a similar way.

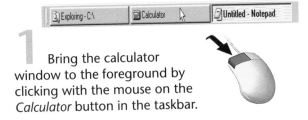

1 Bring the calculator window to the foreground by clicking with the mouse on the *Calculator* button in the taskbar.

Most windows have a *Close* button.

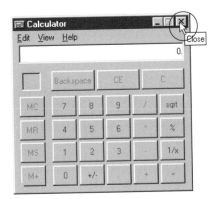

2 Click on the *Close* button in the upper right corner.

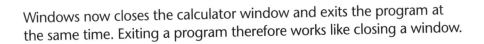

Windows now closes the calculator window and exits the program at the same time. Exiting a program therefore works like closing a window.

Depending on the program, there are other ways to exit.

1 Bring the *Notepad*
window to the foreground.

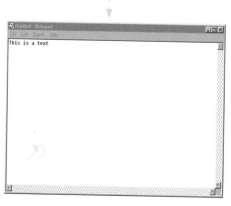

2 Type in any text you like.

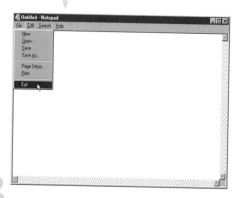

3 Click File in the menu bar
and then click on the Exit command.

Most windows contain an Exit or Close command in their File menu.

If there is still data that you have not saved in the window (e.g. the text you have just typed) then, before exiting, Windows will ask whether you want to save the contents of the window. You will see the dialog box below:

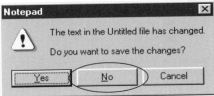

4 Click *No* to exit the program without saving the text you have entered.

> If you have activated the Close function by mistake, choose the *Cancel* button in the above dialog box. This will then bring you back to the application window. You will learn how to save data in the Windows Notepad via the *Yes* button in Chapter 4.

Alternative ways of starting programs

The Start menu allows you to quickly activate a program. Of course there are drawbacks: the program must be installed so that there is an item for it in the Start menu (see also Chapter 11). In addition you might have to open several menus before the program you require appears as an item in the menu. Windows offers you various alternatives for starting programs:

Can you see the icon for the program on the Desktop?

Notepad

1 If so, double-click the program icon.

How to set up a program as an icon on the desktop will be covered in Chapter 11. There we shall also show how programs can be added to or removed from the Start menu.

Windows will then start the associated program immediately. You have already met this (without realising it) when double-clicking the *My Computer* icon. If, for example, the Windows Notepad icon appears on the desktop, all you have to do is double-click it. Straight away Windows opens the Notepad window.

Finally, you can also activate a program directly.

1 Open the Start menu via the Start button.

2 Click the RUN command in the Start menu.

Windows now opens the *Run* dialog box

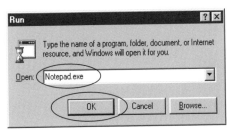

3 Type the name of your program in the *Open* box.

4 Click the OK button.

Windows will now search for this program. If found, it will then be started.

Besides the *Start* button, the taskbar contains other small icons (e.g. a satellite antenna, a stylised letter 'e' etc.). These icons represent buttons and belong to the **Quick Launch** toolbar.

Clicking on a button directly executes the associated program or function. Using the button will zoom out (reduce) all open windows to reveal the desktop. Clicking the icon with the mouse a second time restores the former state. You can also drag other program icons to the Quick Launch toolbar. Windows will then set up the icon in this bar and the program can be started by clicking the mouse on the relevant button.

In Chapter 3 you will learn how to manage files. If a program is displayed as a file in the *My Computer* window or in the Explorer window, it can also be started by double-clicking on the program icon.

3

Managing files and folders

What's in this chapter?

In this chapter you will learn how to manage drives, folders and files. You will find out what types of drive operate with Windows and how diskettes are used for saving data. You will be able to display, copy, delete, move and rename folders and/or files. In addition, we shall show you how to restore files from the Recycle Bin and you will find out how diskettes are formatted and copied.

You already know about:

You are going to learn about:

Folders and files - what are they?

Folders and files are two terms that you will meet frequently in Windows. If they are already familiar to you, you can skip this lesson.

Files are shown in the sub-windows of the *My Computer* window. For example, the window shown here for the *My Documents* **folder** contains the icons of various files.

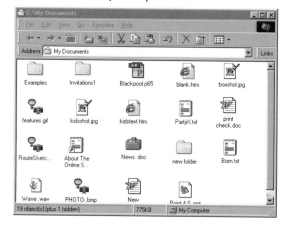

Perhaps you are wondering: **What are files** and why do we need them?

As soon as you use a program to write a letter, to produce a drawing or a picture, to design a spreadsheet table and so on, data will be produced. Of course, in many cases you will not only want to display this data on the screen or print it out, but also store it for later use. In "computer-speak" we say that the data is **saved**; this is done (mostly) on the hard disk or on floppy disks (diskettes).

It is not possible of course to simply store the characters in a letter on a hard disk or diskette. How can the computer or program retrieve a text when there may be several letters on the given **data medium** (hard disk or diskette)? An analogy will help further here: if you were composing a text by hand or with a typewriter, you would staple the pages together in an appropriate manner. Particularly meticulous people would then add a title and, if necessary, a summary in a covering sheet. When storing such a document in an archive, its name and position in the archive would very probably be kept in an index. This allows specific access to the document at a later time.

Something similar happens in a computer. This brings together all related data (e.g. the text of a letter, a picture, a spreadsheet table, a program and so on) into a **file**. You can imagine a file as being a sort of container in which data is packed. Each file receives a name which allows the computer, and ultimately you, to retrieve the file you want.

Rules for filenames

In Windows the **names** for files must satisfy certain rules. A filename may be up to 255 characters long. You may use the letters A to Z, a to z, the figures 0 to 9, the space and various other characters in the name. A valid name would, for example, be *Letter to Miller*. It's not admissible, though, for the characters " / \ | < > to appear in the filename.

In addition to the name, files must also have a **filename extension** (called for short just extension). It consists of a full stop (.), followed by no more than three further letters (e.g. .TXT, .BMP, .EXE, .BAT, .INI, .DOC). These extensions denote the type of file, that is the program with which a file may be edited.

You can write the filename and the extension with large or small letters. Windows makes no distinction between these: so the names "Letter to Miller.doc" and "letter to miller.doc" will be handled identically by Windows. The familiar limits from MS-DOS and Windows 3.1, namely eight characters for the filename and three letters for the extension (often referred to as an 8.3 filename), no longer exist in Windows 95/98 and Windows NT. However, to save unnecessary typing, filenames should be no more than 20 characters long.

Depending on the filename extension, files under Windows will also be allocated different icons. Examples of such filenames are shown below.

Icon	Comment
 Triangle.bmp	This is a graphic file which has the extension *.bmp*. This sort of file can be created and edited using the Windows program *Paint* (see Chapter 4).

67

Display.txt

The notepad icon and the extension *.txt* stand for files containing simple text. You can create such files, for example, with the Windows editor *Notepad* (see Chapter 4).

Chapo1.doc

Chap01.doc

Files with the extension *.doc* likewise contain text, but may also have pictures or specially formatted words or letters (bold, italics etc.). If the upper icon appears in a *.doc* file, it means the file has been produced with the Windows program *WordPad* (see Chapter 4). The lower icon is used if the Windows program *Word* is available on your computer.

Salary.xls

Files with the extension *.xls* contain spreadsheet tables and can be edited with the Windows program *Excel*.

OK.html

Files with the extension *.htm* or *.html* contain Internet documents which can be displayed by Internet Explorer (see Chapter 8).

Edit.hlp

Files with the extension *.hlp* contain help text and are indicated by a book icon. Windows uses these files when you call up the Help function in a program.

Attrib.exe

The extension *.exe* stands for program files. Where these are older MS-DOS programs, the window icon shown opposite is used.

Calc.exe

Windows programs also use the extension *.exe* in filenames. However, in this case, each program will have its own icon (here you see the icon for the Windows Calculator).

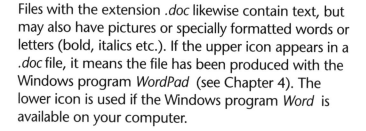

Autoexec.bat

The extension *.bat* is used for certain files containing MS-DOS commands. These files can be run like programs.

TIP

There are many other icons for files, but these depend on the filename extensions and Windows application programs. In your case, maybe Windows doesn't show a filename extension? Refer to the note in Chapter 4 on page 149 in the Section "Saving and loading text" which tells you how to make the extension appear.

There still remains the question: **what are folders and what are they used for?** Once again, an example from everyday office life is helpful. So that we can work better and avoid a "paper chase", letters and documents are filed in folders. A folder includes all documents which are associated in some way.

It is similar for the computer. Files are stored on the hard disk or on diskettes. Open the *My Computer* window and the subwindow for a drive (see the following pages) and Windows will display the files stored on that drive. Like an archive, Windows does this by reading an index and displays the filenames as well as other information.

The window *Chap02* opposite shows an extract with 32 files (in this window also called objects).

It can now be seen that it is difficult to find a particular file straight away. But how would it look if, instead of 32 stored files, you had, say, several thousand?

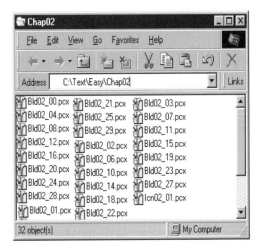

69

In this case it would be very tedious to trace a particular file. It's rather like having to fish out a letter you want from a pile of papers. However, similar to the office, Windows has an elegant solution for storing documents: files that come under the same topic are filed in **folders**.

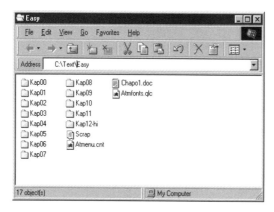

Folders in which files and subfolders can be stored are created on a hard disk or diskette.

The window opposite shows the contents of the folder *Easy*. You will see it has a number of folder icons and various files.

In Windows all folders are represented by a folder icon. This enables you to distinguish files and folders. The criteria you use to split your files into folders remain up to you: files can be organised under particular headings (e.g. you could put all letters in a folder *Letters*, all invoices in a second folder *Invoices* and so on).

Drives under Windows

For storing files and folders we use diskettes, hard disks and CD-ROMs. If, for example, you open the *My Computer* window, then Windows will show the drives available on the computer for these data media. Each drive is identified by its name and an icon.

The icons indicate the type of drive.

3½ Floppy (A:)

5,25- Floppy
[A:]

Both these icons are used for floppy disk drives. The diskette icon indicates which type of diskette the drive supports. In general, new computers only use 3.5-in. diskettes. These are approx 9 cm x 9 cm and housed in a rigid case. Older computers still often use 5.25-in. diskettes that have a diameter of approx 13.5 cm and are encased in a flexible plastic jacket.

Caddy08 (C:)

Hard drives are assigned this icon. This sort of drive is built into the computer and, unlike a diskette, cannot be changed. Considerably more data can be stored on a hard disk than on a diskette.

[D:]

If your computer has a CD-ROM drive, it will be represented by the icon shown here.

71

System [C]

Finally, there is still the question: **How do we name drives?** As soon as the *My Computer* window opens, you will see the icons for the drives on your computer together with a designation for the drive. These drive designations may differ from computer to computer (i.e. Data1 (D:), System (C:) etc.). Nevertheless, all drives are named according to a simple scheme which is valid for all Windows computers:

➡ Drives are enumerated using letters A to Z followed by a colon. You can see these letters in the *My Computer* window.

➡ The **floppy disk drive** is usually considered as the first drive and so will be referred to as the **A:** drive.

➡ If there is a **second floppy disk drive**, this will be given the letter **B:**.

➡ The **first hard disk** is given the letter **C:**.

If there are **further hard disks** and **CD-ROM** drives, they will then be assigned the letters **D:**, **E:**, **F:** to **Z:**.

Handling diskettes

When working on the computer you will probably also make use of diskettes. You can, for example, copy files from the hard disk onto diskettes and then store these in an archive. In addition, programs are still offered for sale on diskette (as well as CD-ROM). You must then install the programs onto the hard disk from diskette (see Chapter 11).

When working with diskettes there are a few points to note. Here you see a 3.5-in. diskette housed in a rigid case.

The sticky label is for labelling the diskette and you should always take hold of a diskette by this label.

The metal slider on the bottom edge protects the magnetic layer of the plastic disk inside the jacket from dust, dirt and fingerprints.

In the top right corner, the diskette has a small rectangular opening that can be closed by a sliding tab. If the opening is closed, files on the diskette can be copied, but when opened it **protects the diskette from being overwritten**. An opening on the left side of the diskette indicates that it is a 1.44 MB diskette, whereas a 720 Kbyte diskette does not have this opening.

To insert the diskette, take hold of it by the label and push it as shown in the illustration (metal slider first and label facing up) until it latches into the drive.

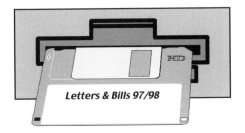

Letters & Bills 97/98

To remove the diskette, press the eject button on the drive.

After removing a diskette from a drive, it should be stored away in a diskette box. Diskettes must not be exposed to dust, fluids, heat or magnetic fields (that is, not in close proximity to telephones, monitors or loudspeakers) as this may lead to loss of data.

73

Displaying drives, files and folders

To display the contents of disk drives, Windows offers you a number of options.

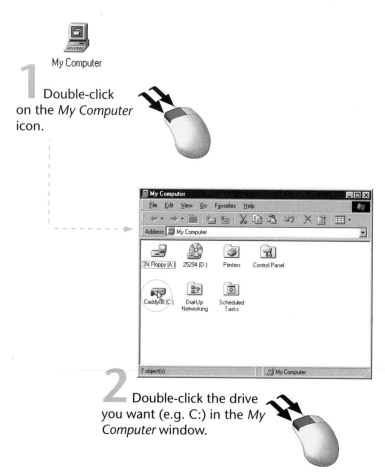

My Computer

1 Double-click on the *My Computer* icon.

2 Double-click the drive you want (e.g. C:) in the *My Computer* window.

A window will now open displaying the contents of the drive. In this window you will see the icons for the files and folders stored on this disk drive.

The other elements in the window such as scroll bars, toolbar and buttons for closing the window will already be familiar to you from Chapter 1.

You can use the scroll bars to scroll in the folder window. Alternatively, you can change the size of the window. Look up the steps for this in Chapter 1.

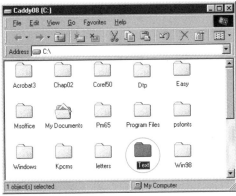

3 Double-click on a folder icon.

Windows now opens the window of the folder required. Here you see the folder *Text* which in turn contains various subfolders and more files.

You open a subfolder window by double-clicking its icon.

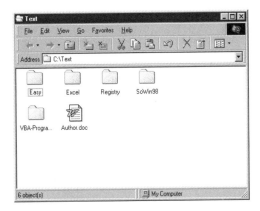

4 To go one step back in the folder hierarchy to the folder above, click the *Up* button in the window.

The buttons *Forward* and *Back* in the toolbar enable you to page between folder windows.

Incidentally, in the window shown opposite you can see the text label window of an application.

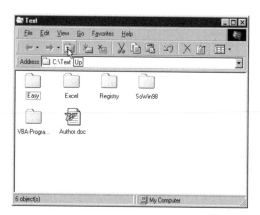

You can also press the ← button to go back to the previous folder in the hierarchy.

Is the toolbar with the buttons missing from your window? Would you like to display it?

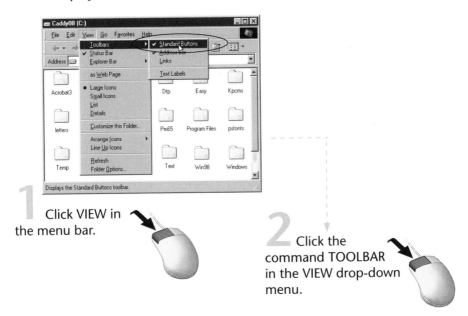

1 Click VIEW in the menu bar.

2 Click the command TOOLBAR in the VIEW drop-down menu.

If the STANDARD BUTTONS entry in the TOOLBAR command submenu is selected (as indicated by a tick), the Standard Buttons toolbar will be displayed.

A second mouse-click on the STANDARD BUTTONS command will remove the toolbar. The other two commands in the submenu toggle in and out the Address Bar toolbar and the Links toolbar for the Internet.

Incidentally, the status bar can be displayed at the bottom of the window via the VIEW menu and the STATUS BAR command; this applies to many windows in Windows applications.

Normally, a text label is displayed in the icons of the Standard *Buttons* toolbar. If the size of the folder window is reduced, there will no longer be enough space on the toolbar to display all the buttons. You then turn off the selection of the command Text Labels in the VIEW/TOOLBAR menu so that Windows can display the button icons more compactly. You will know the name of a button as soon as you position the mouse pointer over the icon, since Windows then displays the Text Label.

Does it bother you that Windows opens a **new window for each folder**? We can easily change this.

1 Open the menu VIEW.

2 With a mouse click choose the command FOLDER OPTIONS.

3 In the FOLDER OPTIONS dialog box, select "Custom, based on settings you choose:" under the *General* tab.

4 Click the Settings button.

5 Click the option "Open each folder in the same window" in the *Custom Settings* dialogue box.

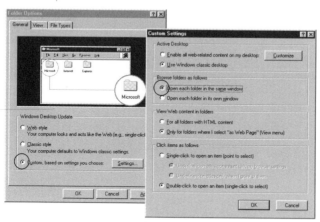

6 Close the dialog box by clicking *OK* and the *General* tab by clicking the *Close* button.

All the open folders are now displayed in the same folder.

It has probably already occurred to you that **different icon sizes** are used in the *My Computer* window and/or in the associated subfolder windows. Some windows use large icons for folders and files, while others have small icons. You can set this via the toolbar.

1 Increase the size of the folder window until you can see all the toolbar buttons.

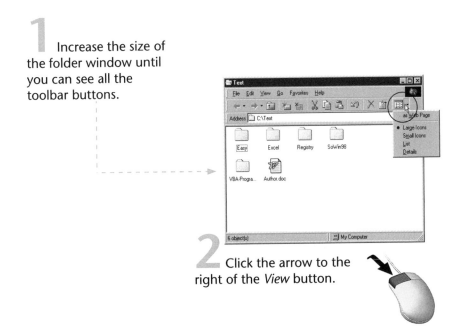

2 Click the arrow to the right of the *View* button.

Windows opens a drop-down menu with options for icon size.

3 Click on the menu item LARGE ICONS.

File and folder icons now appear **large**.

79

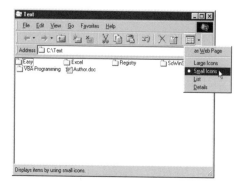

Repeat the above steps, but this time click on SMALL ICONS.

Windows now uses small icons to display files and folders.

Now repeat the above steps but this time click on LIST.

The display in the window is now in the form of a list with the icons and names for files and folders displayed one under the other.

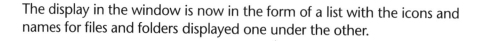

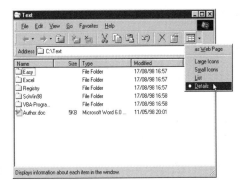

6 Now repeat the above steps but this time click on DETAILS.

The display in the window expands to show information on file size, file type and date of the last change.

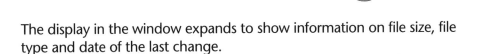

You can also activate these display options via the VIEW menu, where you will find commands with the same names. The current setting is displayed by a full stop (.) before the menu item.

Sorting folders

File and folder icons are sorted and displayed according to given criteria. You can set these sorting criteria via the ARRANGE ICONS command in the VIEW menu.

1 Click on VIEW in the menu bar and then on ARRANGE ICONS.

81

2 To sort the display by name, click on the command BY NAME.

3 Click on the ARRANGE ICONS / BY TYPE commands in the VIEW menu. Windows now sorts the display according to file type (determined by the **filename extension**).

4 Click on the ARRANGE ICONS / BY SIZE commands in the VIEW menu. Windows now sorts the display according to file size.

5 In the VIEW menu, choose the ARRANGE ICONS / BY DATE commands and Windows will sort the display according to the date the file was last changed.

If you have chosen the *Details* display mode, the display can be sorted directly. You only have to click on the column headings to sort the list according to the relevant criterion. In the picture opposite, sorting is in alphabetical order by filename. Clicking the "Name" column heading reverses the sort sequence (e.g. names beginning with Z are now displayed first.)

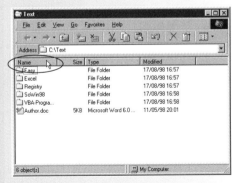

The **desktop** is ultimately nothing more than a folder. You can therefore arrange the icons on the Desktop in the same way.

1 Right-click with the mouse on any free area on the desktop.

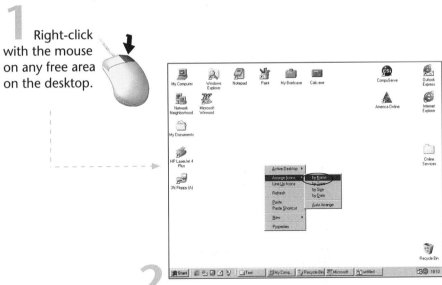

2 Choose the ARRANGE ICONS command in the **context menu** and the desired sorting criterion in the submenu.

Windows then shows the icons on the desktop rearranged according to the chosen sorting criterion.

83

To tidy up the arrangement of the icons on the desktop or in a folder window, you have two options. Choose the command VIEW / LINE UP ICONS and Windows will line up the icons in a folder window or on the desktop as you want. Use the command AUTO ARRANGE in the VIEW / ARRANGE ICONS menu and Windows will line up the icons automatically on the screen. You will not then be able, for example, to drag the icons on the desktop to any position you want: Windows will immediately move them back to their old position. Both commands are barred, however, if the folder window is set to the "Details" display mode.

Click with the right mouse button on any object and Windows will open a menu showing the commands which are directly available (in context); this menu is therefore known as a **context menu**.

Displaying files and folders in Explorer

The icon *My Computer* provides a neat way of displaying the contents of a disk drive or folder. One drawback, however, is the lack of an overview of the folder hierarchy. Windows therefore offers **Explorer** as an alternative for displaying drives, folders and files. You have already started this program in Chapter 2. Can you remember how it works?

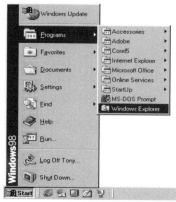

Click on PROGRAMS in the Start menu and in the submenu on the entry WINDOWS EXPLORER.

The program *Explorer* is launched and the window shown opposite opens.

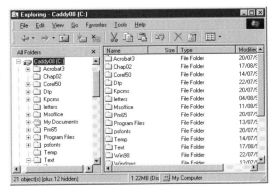

You will already know many elements of this window from the *My Computer* window and its subfolder windows.

The menu bar, toolbar and status bar are the same as in the *My Computer* window, whilst the item TOOLS has been added in the menu bar. In contrast to folders windows, the Explorer window is split.

The **right half** of the **window** shows the same display as the *My Computer* window or a folder window. You will see the icons for folders and files together with their names. You can change how these windows look via the menu bar or toolbar (large or small icons, lists, details or sorted objects) in exactly the same way as has been described on the previous pages.

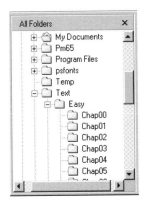

The new feature is the **content of the left pane** of the **Explorer window**. This part is also known as the **Explorer bar.** It shows the drives and the **folder hierarchy** (sometimes called the folder tree). In the illustration on the left, for example, you can see the folder *Text* which in turn contains the subfolder *Easy.* This folder contains further subfolders (*Chap01, Chap02* and *Chap03, etc.*).

If a drive contains a large number of folders, you can use the scroll bar to scroll through the list.

The drive and folder display in the left pane of the window provides you with a quick overview of the drive or folder you are about to work with.

85

1 Click on a drive or folder icon.

Explorer automatically shows its contents in the right pane of the window.

In front of many folder icons you will see a little square with a **minus sign**.

```
   Text
   Easy
      Chap00
      Chap01
      Chap02
      Chap03
```

2 Click on this minus sign and Explorer will remove the **subfolder** icons from the display.

A small **plus sign** in the square in front of the folder icon indicates that the folder has further subfolders.

```
   Text
   Win98
   Windows
```

3 Click on the plus sign and Explorer will display the subfolders at the next level down.

4 By clicking on a drive or folder icon in the left pane you can very quickly change the folders or drives. Explorer will then automatically display the contents of the folder or drive in the right pane of the window.

Incidentally, in the status bar you will see how much storage space a chosen object (drive, folder or file) occupies and how much space is still free on the drive.

Changing drives and folders

With the help of the previous pages you have learnt how the *My Computer* window and Explorer can be used to display files in folders or drives. It is therefore now the right time to check on progress with the aid of a small example.

1 Open the *My Computer* window and select drive C: by double-clicking.

2 Search in the window of the drive C: for the folder in which Windows is stored (usually the *Windows* folder) and open the window to display the folder.

87

3 Search for the *System* folder and open its window by double-clicking on the icon.

4 Now double-click on the icon for the folder *Color*. The window for this folder and its files will now open.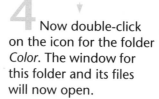

5 Insert a diskette in drive A: and then change to the window **displaying** the **diskette contents**.

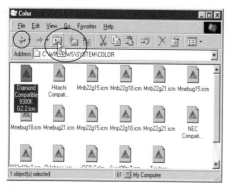

You will have to use the *Up* (or *Back*) button on the toolbar to return to the *My Computer* window and then double-click on the icon of the diskette drive.

Were you able to carry out the above steps without any problem? Then you are already on the way to mastering the most important requirements for working with files. On the following pages you will find further instructions for improving your proficiency with Windows.

But there was another point to the exercise: did you notice how long-winded it was to change from the folder *Color* to the diskette contents? Even changing to a folder at a higher level requires several mouse clicks. In Explorer it is much easier since the left pane shows the icons of the individual folders and drives directly. But maybe you prefer to work with the *My Computer* window? There is a smarter way for changing between folders and drives.

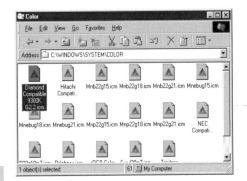

1 Via the *My Computer* icon, change to the Windows folder *Color* on drive C:.

2 Now take a look at the toolbar.

Beneath the toolbar with the buttons you should be able to see another toolbar (**the Address Bar**) with the name of the desired folder.

If you can't see this toolbar, use the ADDRESS BAR command under VIEW / TOOLBARS.

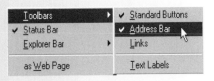

To the right of the **list box** with the designation *Address* you will find a button.

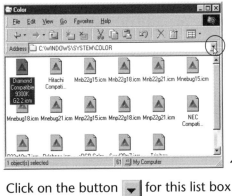

3 Click on the button ▼ for this list box with the mouse.

89

Windows opens the list box, which shows the hierarchy of the currently displayed folder as well as the computer drives that can be accessed from *My Computer*.

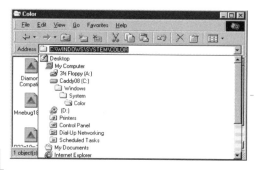

4 If necessary, use the scroll bar until the floppy disk drive can be seen.

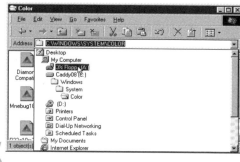

5 Click on the floppy disk drive icon.

Windows will now show directly the contents of this drive in the window.

You will find a list box for changing folders not only in the *My Computer* window and its subwindows, but also in Explorer. Many programs also have dialog boxes for reading or saving data in which you also find a list box. But these will then be labelled *Look in, Save in* and so on instead of *Address*.

Creating a new folder

To create a new folder on a drive or in an existing folder, proceed in the following manner:

1 Open the window for the drive or folder.

2 **Right-click** with the mouse on any free area of the window.

Windows will now open a **context menu** with the commands that are available.

3 Point to the command NEW. - - - - - - - ▶

91

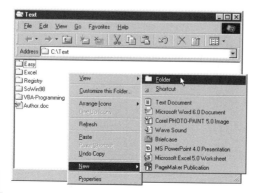

4 Choose the command
FOLDER in the submenu.

Windows creates a new folder
with the name *New Folder* in
the window. The name of this
new folder is selected in colour,
which means you can still
change its name.

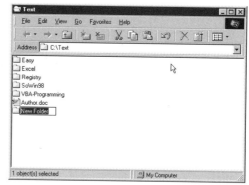

5 Type in the new name for the
folder using the keyboard.

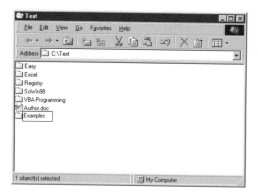

In the window on the left,
Examples has been chosen as
the name. You can, however,
use any valid folder name.

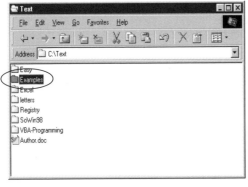

 Click on any free area of the window.

Windows cancels the selection and assigns the keyed name to the new folder.

You can create new folders in the *My Computer* window and its subfolder windows. But not only there: in the right pane of Explorer you can follow the same steps to create a folder. The desktop is ultimately a permanently open folder which means that you can take the steps for creating a new folder on the desktop too. Even in applications like *WordPad* or *Paint*, it is possible to make use of commands for creating a new folder within the dialog boxes for saving files (see Chapter 4).

Creating a new file

In most cases you will produce files using text programs, drawing programs and so on (see Chapter 4). At the beginning of this chapter it was mentioned that there are different file types (for graphics, text etc.). These programs automatically ensure that the relevant file types are used for new files. Windows nevertheless lets you create empty files of certain file types without calling up application programs so you can, for example, create a model for a letter or an empty text document (the advantages will become clear in Chapter 5).

1 Right-click with the mouse on any free area of the window.

2 Point the mouse in the context menu on the command NEW and then select the desired file type (e.g. TEXT DOCUMENT).

3 Type in the name you want for the new file.

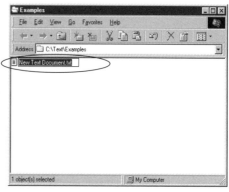

4 Click any free area of the window. Windows will create a new file with the required name.

When creating a new file or folder, at the start you often click on another area in the window before entering the name. Windows then uses the default name for the new folder or file. In the next lesson you will see how the name of a file or folder can be changed at a later stage.

When entering the new filename, the previously assigned filename extension is easily changed. However, Windows uses this extension for recognising file types.

If this warning appears, close the message box by clicking the *No* button and type in the name together with the filename extension.

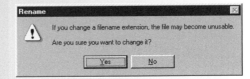

Renaming folders and files

The names of files and folders can also be changed very easily at a later stage:

1 **Right-click** with the mouse on the icon of the folder or file to be renamed.

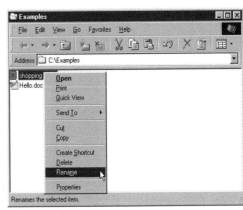

2 In the context menu, choose the command RENAME.

95

Windows selects the name of the folder or file.

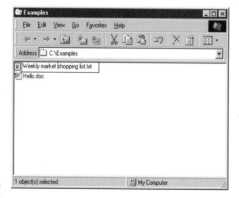

3 Type in the new name.

4 Left-click with the mouse on any free area of the desktop.

Windows then changes the name of the folder or file.

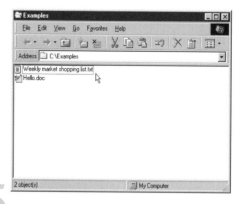

5 Now click a second time on any free area of the window to cancel the selection.

You can also change the name by selecting a file or folder and then pressing the function key F3.

Windows allows the filename to be displayed with or without its extension. In this book we shall display filename extensions. When renaming files the problem mentioned in the previous lesson will then arise: the filename extension must be maintained. Unfortunately the RENAME command selects the complete filename together with the filename extension. Typing in the first few letters of the new name causes the previous name to disappear (with its extension). However, there is a trick for just changing the filename or part of it. As soon as the mouse pointer is over the selected area, it assumes this form: Ⲓ. This symbol is also called a **text cursor**. It indicates that text may be edited.

1 shopping list.txt

Click on the first character of the name. The position will now be indicated by a flashing vertical line (the **insertion point**).

2 Weekly market shopping list shopping list.txt

If you now type in some letters, these will appear at the position of the insertion point. At the same time the old name will be pushed to the right.

The question still remains: how can you remove the superfluous characters of the old name? Characters to the right of the insertion point may be deleted with the Delete key. Characters to the left of the text cursor can be deleted with the ← key. In addition, the cursor keys ← and → can be used to move the insertion point in the text.

You should make a note of these keys since they are extremely useful for all text input. This will become particularly clear when writing letters and other texts in Chapter 4.

Copying folders and files

Files can be copied between folders on the hard disk or between the hard disk and a floppy disk. Take for instance a letter that is to be saved for later use. Copy the file containing the letter onto a diskette and store the diskette safely. Would you like to use the text of a letter as a model for a new letter without changing the original? A copy of the file with the letter stored under a new name in a folder will solve the problem.

Windows offers you many options for copying files or complete folders together with the files they contain. In the following, you will become familiar with the most important steps for copying files and folders. In the first example a file will be transferred onto a diskette.

Open the *My Computer* window by double-clicking its icon.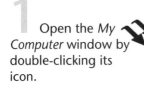

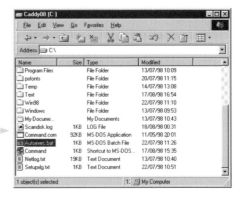

Double-click the icon for drive C: and search on this disk drive for the file *Autoexec.bat*.

The simplest way to do this is to choose the *Details* display mode.

3 Insert an empty, but **formatted, diskette** in floppy disk drive A: (tips for formatting diskettes can be found at the end of this chapter).

4 Double click on the *My Computer* icon to open a second window.

5 Now double-click on the icon for floppy disk drive A:.

6 Position both open windows alongside each other.

7 Whilst holding down the right mouse button, drag the *Autoexec.bat* file from its original window into the second window of the floppy disk drive.

8 Release the right mouse button as soon as the file icon is over the window.

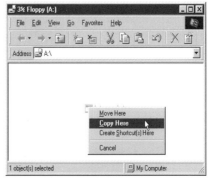

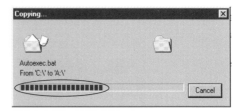

9 From the context menu, choose the command COPY HERE.

Windows then copies the file into the window indicated (and hence onto the diskette). During the copying operation progress is also indicated in a small window.

Before using a diskette for the first time, it must be appropriately prepared: this process is called **formatting**. This involves creating a **file allocation table** on the diskette. Windows enters the names of the folders and files that are saved on the diskette into this table. Many diskettes that you buy are already preformatted by the manufacturer. However, you can also format diskettes yourself. You will see how to do this in the lesson "Formatting diskettes" at the end of this chapter.

Did Windows display an error message and refuse to copy onto the diskette? Perhaps the diskette is write-protected. You must then remove the write protection (see the lesson "Handling diskettes" in this chapter).

1 Repeat the last steps and copy the file *Autoexec.bat* onto the diskette again.

When copying, Windows will establish that a file of the same name already exists on the diskette. The **dialog box** opposite will then be displayed. Cancel the copying operation by clicking the *No* button.

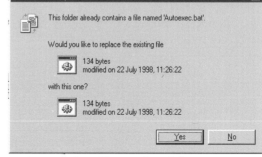

If you choose the *Yes* button, Windows will copy over the existing file on the diskette.

Windows lets you not only copy files and folders between hard disk and diskette or to other drives, but it is also possible to copy files and folders between different folders in the same drive. To do this, simply open both windows for the two folders. The folder in which the files are contained is called the **source folder**, and the folder into which the files are to be copied is the **destination folder**.

Copying several files at the same time

If you want to copy several files, the method described in the foregoing section is rather long-winded. In this lesson a number of files will be **copied** at once from the folder *Examples* into the folder *Letters*.

1 Open the window for drive C: and create two new folders *Examples* and *Letters*.

2 Open the window for the folder *Examples* and create some text files.

3 Open the folder *Letters* in a second window.

We have already shown you on the previous pages how to create folders and files and open a folder window. Now you need a method that will enable you to **select** several files for copying:

1 Arrange the two windows side by side.

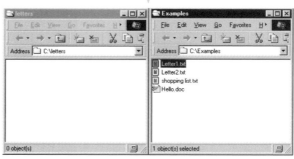

2 Click in the folder *Examples* on the first of the files to be copied.

To select several consecutive files, proceed as follows:

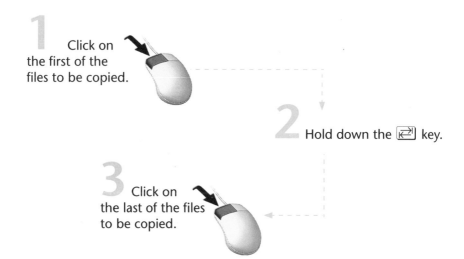

1 Click on the first of the files to be copied.

2 Hold down the ⇥ key.

3 Click on the last of the files to be copied.

103

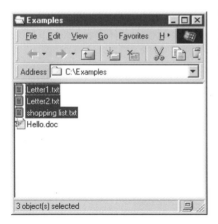

Windows will now select all the files in between. This is shown by the coloured background to the filenames.

Perhaps you want to select several files that are not next to one another?

1 Hold down the
`Ctrl` key.

2 Now click on the files to be selected.

104

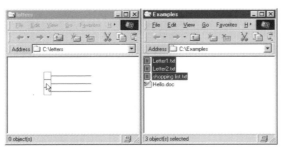

3 To copy, this time right-click with the mouse on the files, keep the button depressed and drag the selected files to the window with the destination folder. Now release the mouse button again.

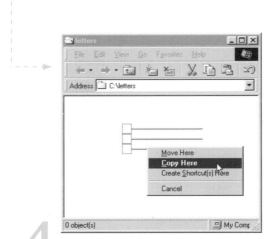

4 In the context menu that is now open, choose the command COPY HERE.

In addition to files, you can of course also select folders and copy them into another folder by dragging with the mouse.

Windows will now copy the selected files from the source folder to the destination folder. Usually, copying between folders on the hard disk happens so quickly that the *Copying* dialog box indicating progress is not displayed.

Copying a file in the same folder

Would you like to use a file containing perhaps the text of a letter as a basis for a new letter, but keep the original file? Then it would seem sensible to make a copy of the file concerned and work with this copy. Unfortunately there is one small problem: you cannot copy in the same folder by dragging with the mouse. Furthermore, when copying, you must ensure that the new file has a different name from the original file (filenames must be unique within a folder). However, there is a method for copying that also works within a folder.

1   Select the file to
be copied.

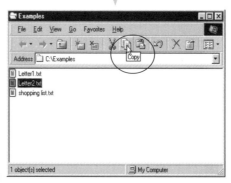

2   Click on the *Copy* button in
the window toolbar.

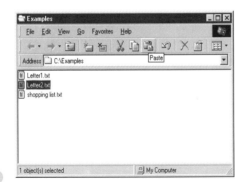

3 Click on the *Paste* button in the window toolbar.

Windows pastes a copy of the selected file into the active folder.

At the same time the name of the new file is changed so as to distinguish it from the original file. *Copy from xxx* is used for the new name, where xxx indicates the old filename. If required, you can of course rename the copied file.

Windows has three functions for cutting, copying and pasting selected areas (text, files, graphics etc.). Cut or copied areas are then placed into a background area of temporary storage called the **clipboard**. When pasting, Windows transfers the content of the clipboard and pastes it into the current window.

 Using this button, a selected area can be cut out and transferred to the clipboard. The cut area disappears from the active window. Alternatively, you can use the key combination $Ctrl$ and X to cut out a selected area.

 This button copies the selected area onto the clipboard. The content of the active window is not changed. Alternatively, you can use the key combination $Ctrl$+C to copy a selected area.

 This button pastes the content of the clipboard back into the active window. This can be used to transfer text, pictures and files. Alternatively, you can use the key combination $Ctrl$+V to paste a selected area.

107

Moving folders and files

When copying in the same folder or between folders or disk drives, you
will have two files with the same content. Sometimes, however, a file is
only to be moved from one folder to another folder. A file will therefore
be created in the destination folder while being simultaneously deleted
from the source folder. This works in a similar way to copying.

1 Open the folder
window containing
the file.

2 Open the folder
window into which the file
is to be moved.

3 Arrange the two
windows side by side.

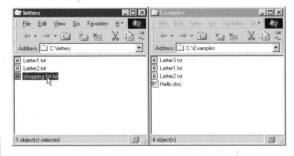

4 Select the file(s) to be
moved by clicking with the
mouse.

5 Keeping the right mouse button depressed, drag the selected file(s) from the source window to the destination window.

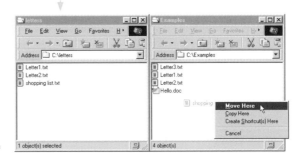

6 Release the mouse button and choose the command COPY HERE in the context menu.

Windows now moves the selected file(s) into the destination folder. The file will now be deleted from the source folder.

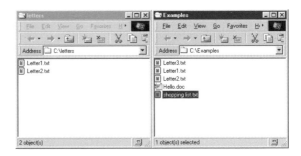

As with copying, you can select and move several files. If there is already a file with one of these filenames in the target folder, Windows asks whether you want to replace it by the file to be moved.

109

Copying diskettes

Many folders and files can be stored on a diskette (floppy disk). Using Windows, you can copy the contents of a complete diskette onto a second diskette.

1 Insert the diskette with your data into the floppy disk drive.

2 Open the *My Computer* window.

3 Right-click with the mouse on the floppy disk drive icon.

4 In the context menu, choose the command COPY DISK.

Windows displays the *Copy Disk* dialog box.

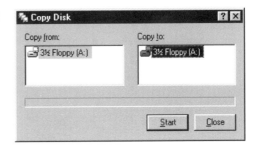

5 If you have several floppy disk drives, you can choose the source and destination floppy disk drives by clicking.

6 Click on the *Start* button to start the copying operation.

Windows reads in the data from the source diskette and informs you of progress in a display.

Once the data has been read, Windows invites you to change the diskette.

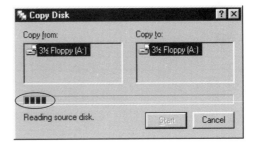

7 Remove the source diskette from the drive and insert the empty destination diskette.

111

8 Click on the *OK* button.

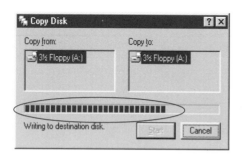

Windows now writes the data onto the new (destination) diskette. The dialog box opposite informs you about progress.

Once copying of the diskette has finished an appropriate message appears.

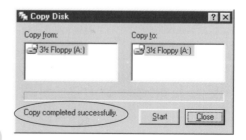

9 Close the dialog box via the *Close button*.

10 Remove the diskette from the drive.

You now have an exact copy of the original diskette.

> When copying, the destination diskette is overwritten. Any data on this diskette will be lost. Also, you can only copy between two data media that are the same. Copying from a 3.5 in. diskette to a 5.25 in. will not work in this way. The same applies if you want to copy a 3.5 in. diskette of 720 Kbyte capacity to a 1.44 MB diskette.

How much is stored on a disk drive?

Would you like to know how much data is already stored on a diskette or hard disk? Are you interested in how much data will still fit on the drive (this is also known as the **capacity**)?

1 Open the *My Computer* window.

2 Right-click on the icon for the disk drive concerned.

3 In the context menu, choose the command PROPERTIES.

113

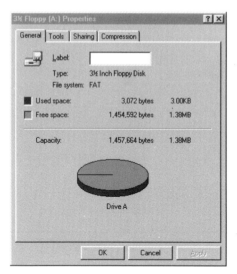

Windows opens the window shown opposite to display the **properties** dialog box for the **disk drive**. Under the *General* tab you will find information such as how many bytes still remain on the drive and how much space has already been used up.

The illustration here shows that a drive with a 1.44 MB diskette has been selected.

How much storage space does a folder or file occupy?

Would you like to know how many files are stored in a folder and how much storage space they use up? This would be important if, for example, you wanted to copy all the files in a folder onto a diskette.

1 Open the window in which the folder is displayed.

2 **Right-click** with the mouse button on the icon for the folder concerned.

3 In the context menu, choose the command PROPERTIES.

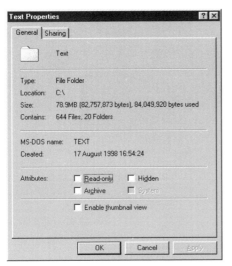

Windows opens a window displaying the properties of the folder. Here you will see how many subfolders and files the selected file contains. At the same time you can see how much storage space these files use up.

The size of files appears directly in the display if, for example, you choose the *Details* display mode in the Explorer window. As for a folder, you can also select the file and choose the command PROPERTIES in the context menu. The properties window for files is shown here. You can find out not only how large the file is but also when it was last changed.

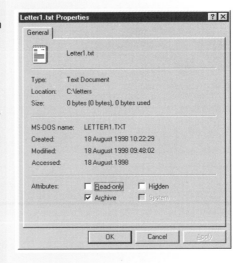

115

Deleting files and folders

Are there folders or files you no longer need? If so, you can easily delete them.

1 Open the folder window containing the file or folder.

2 Select the file or folder to be deleted.

3 Holding down the left mouse button, drag the file or folder to be deleted to the Recycle Bin.

4 As soon as the mouse pointer is over the Recycle Bin release the left mouse button.

Windows will now move the selected file(s) or folder(s) into the Recycle Bin.

Although the above method is very convenient, there is a drawback: sometimes the Recycle Bin is hidden by other windows. In this case there are two further methods you can use for deleting files or folders.

1 Open the window displaying the folder or file.

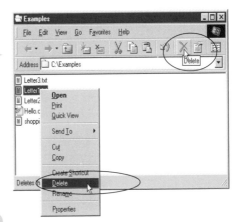

2 Right-click the file or folder you want to delete and in the context menu choose the command DELETE.

3 Or select the file and click on the *Delete* button.

For security, when deleting, Windows enquires whether you really want to delete the object (file/folder).

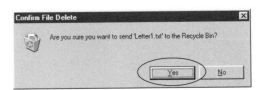

117

4 Click the *Yes* button in the
Confirm File [Delete] dialog box.

The selected object will now be moved to the Recycle Bin.

Retrieving deleted files from the Recycle Bin

Have you accidentally deleted a file or folder that you still need? So long as the file(s) is/are still in the Recycle Bin you will be able to retrieve them. To retrieve a deleted file there are two possibilities.

If you notice the mistake at the time of deletion then retrieval is quite easy.

1 Right-click with
the mouse on any free
area of the window with
a view of the folders or
files.

 In the context menu, choose the command UNDO DELETE.

Windows will now retrieve the last deleted file from the Recycle Bin into the active window.

 However, this method only works if you have not done anything else. The menu item UNDO always refers to the last executed Windows command. If the file is no longer in the Recycle Bin, the command UNDO DELETE will be blocked and so you will not be able to choose it.

 In the toolbar of the window you will find the button which also undoes the last command. If a file has just been deleted, this button retrieves it from the Recycle Bin.

If you have carried out several steps and do not realise the mistake until later, there is another method with which you might still be able to "rescue" the deleted files.

119

Recycle Bin

1 Double-click on the Recycle Bin icon.

2 Select the deleted file(s) in the Recycle Bin window.

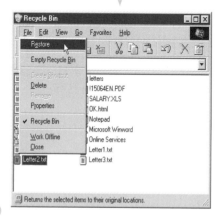

3 In the FILE menu choose the command RESTORE.

Windows will now move the selected file(s) back into the original folder.

Emptying the Recycle Bin

When deleting a file or folder, Windows only moves the object to the Recycle Bin. Although the file or folder will then disappear from the active window, the **storage space** required for the files on the drive will still be reserved. Although Windows does check whether the Recycle Bin is "full" and automatically removes those files recorded as having been deleted the longest time ago, you can assist by **emptying** the **Recycle Bin** yourself from time to time.

1 Right-click with the mouse on the Recycle Bin icon.

Open
Explore
Empty Recycle Bin
Create Shortcut
Properties

2 In the context menu, choose the command EMPTY RECYCLE BIN.

Windows asks whether you really want to delete the items in the Recycle Bin.

Confirm Multiple File Delete	✕
Are you sure you want to delete these 18 items?	
Yes	No

3 Click on the *Yes* button.

Once you have emptied the Recycle Bin, the deleted files will be gone for good.

The files are removed from the Recycle Bin. At the same time the disk storage space reserved for the files is released. The icon of an empty Recycle Bin will now appear.

121

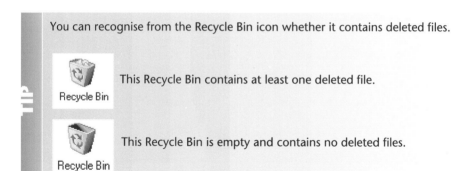

You can recognise from the Recycle Bin icon whether it contains deleted files.

This Recycle Bin contains at least one deleted file.

This Recycle Bin is empty and contains no deleted files.

Finding files and folders

Have you forgotten in which folder you put a file or subfolder? Windows will help you search for a file or folder.

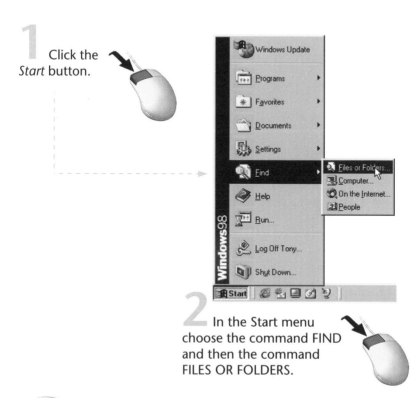

Click the *Start* button.

In the Start menu choose the command FIND and then the command FILES OR FOLDERS.

Windows displays the window for entering the search requirements.

3 Enter the search
requirements and click
Find Now.

The name of the file or folder to find is entered in the box *Named.*

➡ If you know the name exactly, you will be able to enter it in full.

➡ Often, however, it is the case that the exact written form is not known. Perhaps you only know that the file begins with *Letter.* In this case enter just the beginning of the name in the box *Named.* All files and folders beginning with these characters will then be listed in the results area of the window *Find.*

➡ If you want to limit the search to a particular file type, you can use a search term in the form *Letter*.txt.* The star is called a **wildcard**, i.e. the * character represents any letters in the name: one or more letters may be substituted. The results window will then display files with names such as *Letter.txt, Letter3.txt, Letter to Miller.txt, Letters.txt.* The folder *Letters* will not be displayed as it does not have the specified filename extension *.txt.* Neither will *My Letter.txt* be found as the search pattern does not match.

123

In the box *Containing text* you can enter a keyword contained in the file. The search function will then check whether this keyword occurs in the file.

In the box *Look in* you have to specify the drive and/or folder to search in. This is a so-called **combination field**: the drive letter and the folder name can be directly typed into the field.

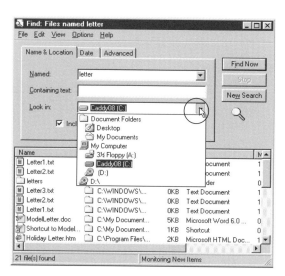

By clicking the  button, you can open a drop-down list box from which to select drives and/or folders.

If you find entering folder names is too much effort, make use of the *Browse* button in the *Find* window. You can then select the drive and the folder in the dialog box *Browse for Folder*. This works like selecting a folder in an Explorer window. As soon as you close the dialog box with the *OK* button, the folder you require will be entered into the *Look in* box.

Do you want Windows to also browse through the subfolders of a drive or folder for the name? If so, make sure the "Include subfolders" check box in the *Find* dialog box is selected with a check mark (otherwise click the check box).

After clicking *Find Now,* Windows will search through the drives and/or folders for the search term, listing the files or folders found in the results area of the *Find* dialog box.

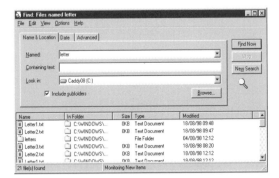

A folder name is preceded by the character \. The folder *Letters* on the *C:* drive will then be specified as *C:\Letters*. The subfolder *Personal* in the folder *Letters* will therefore be specified as *C:\Letters\Personal.* If you use the *Browse* button, you don't have to worry about the format of this; Windows takes care of the composition of names. An entry like *C:\Letters\Personal* is also called a **path** or **pathname** because it specifies the route (or path) to a folder. Such pathnames appear in Windows every time files are accessed. If you wish, the \ character (also termed **backslash**) can be entered directly from the keyboard.

The *Find* function can be directly activated via the [F3] function key if the desktop, a folder window or the Explorer window is open.

125

Formatting diskettes

Before you can use a new diskette you first have to format it. Basically, this involves Windows in creating an index (file allocation table) on the diskette for recording the names of folders and files. During this operation Windows will also check the diskette for any faults.

CAUTION You can of course also reformat a diskette that is already formatted. But if you do this all information stored on the diskette will be lost.

TIP When you buy diskettes, they will often already be preformatted by the manufacturer for use with Windows/MS-DOS. This is indicated by information such as "Formatted", "DOS formatted", "Preformatted" on the diskette packaging. You can then omit the formatting operation before using the diskettes.

To format new diskettes, carry out the following steps:

1 Insert the new diskette into the floppy disk drive, taking care not to activate the write-protect tab

2 Open the *My Computer window*

3 Right-click with the mouse on the floppy disk drive icon.

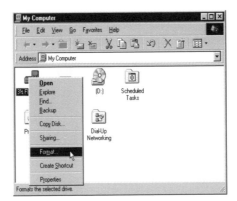

 In the context menu, choose the command FORMAT.

Windows opens the dialog box for formatting the diskette. You can set various options in this dialog box.

 Click on the *Start* button.

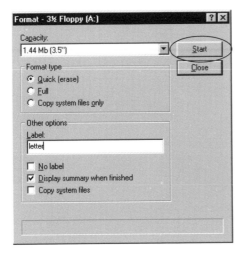

In the list box *Capacity*, you can choose between two different storage densities for the diskette type. The amount of data stored on a 3.5 in. diskette can be either 720 Kbyte or 1.44 MB. If you are formatting a 1.44 MB diskette, more data can be stored on it.

Under the group "Format type" you can choose how you want to format the diskette.

127

If required, you can specify a name (up to eleven characters) in the *Label* field for the diskette.

The "Full" formatting option for a diskette takes some time.

In the bottom half of the dialog box Windows tells you how the formatting operation is progressing.

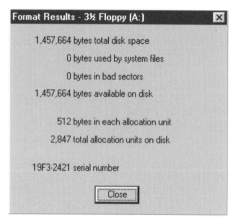

If the check box "Display summary when finished" is selected, Windows will display detailed information on the diskette in this window on completion of formatting.

 Close the message field by means of the *Close* button.

 Click *Close* to leave the formatting dialog box.

The diskette can now be used for storing files and folders.

Displaying a folder as a Web page

Windows 98 possesses built-in functions to directly access documents in the Internet format. This also works for documents on the local hard disk. Thus the folder display can also be selected as a Web page.

1 Open a folder window.

2 In the VIEW menu, choose the command AS WEB PAGE.

> If you choose the command AS WEB PAGE in the VIEW menu again, the folder display will revert to the classic style.

Windows will then display the folder as a Web page. Click on an icon in the window to display its description in the left part of the window.

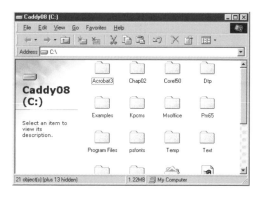

In the VIEW menu, choose the command FOLDER OPTIONS to display the *Folder options* properties window. Select the option *Web style* in the *General* tab and then close the tab via the *OK* button and Windows will switch the display to Web style. The folder display behaves rather like a Web document in Internet Explorer (see Chapter 8). By contrast, the option *Classical style* will switch the display back to the style described in this book.

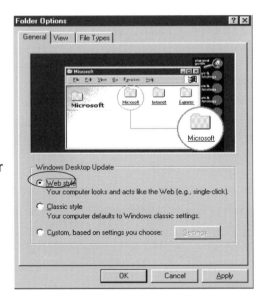

You can recognise Web style by underlined icons. Point to an icon with the mouse and the pointer will assume the form of a hand.

In Web style there is no longer double-clicking. On pointing, Windows selects an object. To activate, you use a single mouse click instead of double-clicking.

 Since this form of operation is quite unfamiliar to users converting to Windows 98, Web style is turned off on installing Windows. For this reason, this book avoids going into a detailed discussion.

Quick progress check

Have you worked through the first three chapters? If so, you've already mastered the basics of working with Windows. The following chapters deal with special points on individual programs and functions. As a check on your knowledge so far, you may like to work through the following questions. After each question we give the lesson where you can find the answer.

➡ How would you get a window to fill the whole screen?

_____

(Answer in Chapter 1 in the Lesson "Working with windows")

➡ How do you exit a program?

_____

(Answer in Chapter 1 in the Lesson "Working with windows"
or in Chapter 2 in "Exiting a program")

➡ Give the alternative ways of starting (launching) a program.

_____

(Answer in Chapter 1 in the Lesson "Starting a program"
or in "Alternative ways of starting programs")

➡ How can a program (.EXE file) be started from the *My Computer* window or in Explorer?

_____

(Answer in Chapter 2 in the tip at the end of the Lesson
"Alternative ways of starting programs")

➡ **How are data files named?**

_____

(Answer in Chapter 3 in the Lesson "Folders and files - what are they?")

➡ **How can you find out what files are stored on a floppy disk?**

_____

(Answer in Chapter 3 in the Lesson "Displaying drives, files and folders")

➡ **How can large icons be displayed in the _My Computer_ window?**

_____

(Answer in Chapter 3 in the Lesson "Displaying drives, files and folders")

➡ **How would you copy a file or folder?**

_____

(Answer in Chapter 3 in the Lesson "Copying files and folders")

➡ **How is a file deleted?**

_____

(Answer in Chapter 3 in the Lesson "Deleting files and folders")

Were you able to answer the questions without any problems?

Fine, now you've mastered the most important basics of Windows. If there's still a problem in some areas, it's not really too serious. If necessary, just look up how it's done in the appropriate lesson. Many operations are similar in Windows which means you will learn a lot as you go along by working through the following chapters.

What's in this chapter ?

Using Windows, you can enter simple text and save it to a file for printing and later use, look at document files supplied with other programs and also format your text rather more attractively, producing letters, invitations, invoices and so on with a personal touch. In addition, Windows enables you to produce and edit sketches, drawings and pictures and use them in documents or as a desktop background. In this chapter you will become acquainted with the Windows programs concerned.

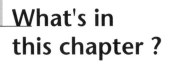

You already know about:

You are going to learn about:

Creating text files with the editor

Would you like to **create simple texts** such as lists, notices or instructions? Instead of writing these by hand or on a typewriter, you can produce them on the computer. Texts like these can be very easily saved for later use and amended if necessary. Printouts look smart and you can print a number of copies of such documents without any problem. To produce a simple text use the **Windows editor**.

1 In the Start menu click on PROGRAMS / ACCESSORIES.

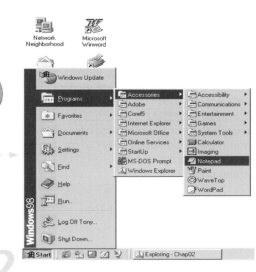

2 Now choose EDITOR with a single mouse click.

Windows will now start the editor.

In the computer world, a program which can be used to create simple text files is called an **editor**. The program Windows uses is an editor called *Notepad.exe* which is stored in the Windows folder.

The Windows editor opens a window like other Windows programs. This window contains elements such as the title bar, menu bar and scroll bars which you already know from other windows in previous chapters.

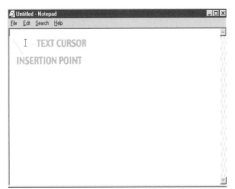

The white **area inside the window** is different: this is where we **enter the text**. When activated, the editor displays a "white page" with no text. In the top left corner of the window you can see the **insertion point**.

The **insertion point** is shown as a vertical flashing black line. This mark indicates where the next character you enter will be inserted on the screen. As soon as the entered character is displayed, the insertion point moves one place to the right. In Windows, insertion points are used wherever text is to be input. For example, you have already met this in Chapter 3 when renaming files.

When you point to the text area, the **text cursor** we have already mentioned appears instead of the mouse pointer. This is manipulated in exactly the same way as the insertion point. You can use the text cursor to point to a word and to select or click something. When you click in text, the text cursor becomes the insertion point.

Here is an example of text that has been entered with the editor.

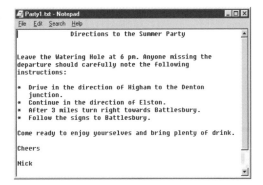

If you're still not familiar with the **operation of the keyboard,** here are a few tips for entering text.

→ To input the first line, first press the key. This will make the insertion point jump a little way to the right. Now type in some text. Using the ⇥ key will move the text to the right (sometimes this is called **indenting**). Instead of the ⇥ you can also use the space bar in the editor to indent the text by several spaces at the start of a line.

→ Normally, on pressing letter keys, lowercase (non-capitalised) letters appear. To **input a capital letter,** keep the ⇧ key held down and then press the letter key you require.

→ When you reach the right margin, the text is pushed to the left in the editor. To end a line at a particular place and **advance to the next line**, press the ↵ (Return) key.

→ If you need more **space between two lines**, press the ↵ key twice; this has been done in the above example between the heading and the following line of text.

See the start of the book for an overview of the keys.

Why not try typing in the above text in the editor? You will soon get a feel for entering text.

Editing text in the editor

When **entering text** you are bound to make **mistakes**. If you want to **revise** a text saved in another document, this will also involve editing.

In our haste we have put in a few mistakes and made various omissions in the Directions to the Summer Party shown here. We shall now correct these step by step. This will be an opportunity for you to get to know some more methods for editing text documents.

To begin with, we have to insert the date when the party is to take place.

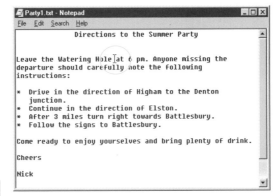

 1 Click with the mouse on the second line before the word "at".

2 Now type in the date.

As you type, the editor moves the text to the right of the insertion point.

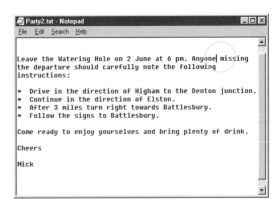

Here you can see the window with the result.

 **3** To adjust the **length of the line**, click after the word "Anyone" and press the ⏎ key.

139

```
Party3.txt - Notepad
File  Edit  Search  Help

                Directions to the Summer Party

Leave the Watering Hole on 2 June at 6 pm. Anyone
missing the departure should carefully note the following
 instructions:

*  Drive in the direction of Higham to the Denton junction.
*  Continue in the direction of Elston.
*  After 3 miles turn right towards Battlesbury.
*  Follow the signs to Battlesbury.

Come ready to enjoy yourselves and bring plenty of drink.

Cheers

Nick
```

4 Click at the start of the third line and delete the space in front of the word "missing".

5 Click with the text cursor at the end of the third line after "following", and press the ⏎ key.

6 Click in the fourth line before the word "instructions" and delete the space at the start of the line by pressing the ⌐Delete⌐ key.

The ⌐Delete⌐ key always **erases characters** to the right of the insertion point. To remove a character to the left of the insertion point, press the ⏎ key.

You can position the insertion point anywhere in the text by clicking with the mouse before the particular letter. However, you can also use the **cursor keys** as well as other keys to move the insertion point in the text. The following overview contains a list of the most important keys and key combinations for moving the insertion point in the text.

Moves the insertion point in
the text one line up.

Moves the insertion point in
the text one line down.

Moves the insertion point in the text one
character to the left towards the start of
the text.

Moves the insertion point in the text one
character to the right towards the end of
the text.

 +

Moves the insertion point in the
text one word to the left.

Moves the insertion point in the
text one word to the right.

 +

Pressing this key causes the insertion
point to jump to the start of the line.

Pressing this key causes the insertion
point to jump to the end of the line.

141

In existing texts it often happens that complete sentences or sections of text have to be deleted. To do this you can set the insertion point at the beginning of the text area and then hold down the [Delete] key until all the characters have been deleted. Deletion can be done more elegantly, however, if you **select** the text.

Selection can be compared with highlighting text in colour on a sheet of paper when you draw a coloured marker over the relevant passages. In the Windows editor you use the mouse pointer by dragging it over the text to be marked.

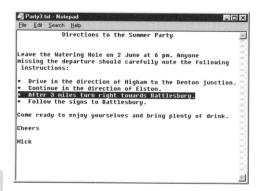

1 Click the mouse at the start of the area of text to be selected.

2 Hold down the left mouse button and drag the mouse to the end of the selected area.

The selected text is highlighted in colour. If you now press the [Delete] key, the editor will delete the entire section of selected text.

To cancel a selection, click anywhere outside the selected area.

You can also use the keyboard to select text. Move the insertion point to the beginning of the area you want to select. Then hold down the [⇧] key and move the insertion point in the text using the keys described above. The editor then selects the characters.

If you deleted something by mistake, you can press the key combination [Ctrl]+[Z], and the **last change** will be **undone**.

Finally, the question arises as to how larger text passages in a document can be moved or copied. This is extremely useful when transferring texts that already exist.

In this window a complete line has been selected which is to be moved to the paragraph above.

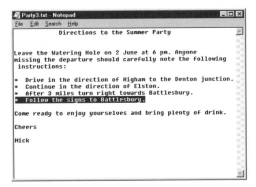

In the EDIT menu, choose the command CUT or press the key combination [Ctrl] + [X].

This text is now deleted from the editor window. Windows has transferred the selected text to the **clipboard**.

143

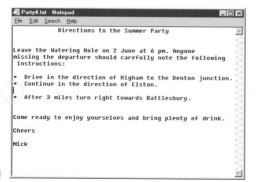

Directions to the Summer Party

Leave the Watering Hole on 2 June at 6 pm. Anyone
missing the departure should carefully note the following
 instructions:

* Drive in the direction of Higham to the Denton junction.
* Continue in the direction of Elston.
* After 3 miles turn right towards Battlesbury.

Come ready to enjoy yourselves and bring plenty of drink.

Cheers

Nick

2 Click after the text "in the direction of Elston" and then insert a new line by means of the ⏎ key.

3 Make sure that the insertion point is at the start of the new line.

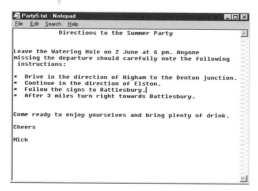

Directions to the Summer Party

Leave the Watering Hole on 2 June at 6 pm. Anyone
missing the departure should carefully note the following
 instructions:

* Drive in the direction of Higham to the Denton junction.
* Continue in the direction of Elston.
* Follow the signs to Battlesbury.
* After 3 miles turn right towards Battlesbury.

Come ready to enjoy yourselves and bring plenty of drink.

Cheers

Nick

4 In the EDIT menu, choose the command PASTE or press the key combination Ctrl + V .

The editor now pastes the **text** on the **clipboard** into the document at the **insertion point**. By means of these steps you have, in effect, moved the previously selected text to the new position.

WHAT'S THIS?

Windows has a specific storage area called the clipboard.
When you choose the functions CUT or COPY (e.g. in the
EDIT menu), Windows places the selected area (text, picture
sections, filename etc.) on the clipboard. Using the PASTE
command in the EDIT menu will then insert the clipboard
contents into the active window.

If you just want to copy a text passage (and retain the selected section),
then similar steps can be used.

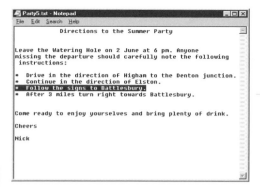

1 Select the section of
text to be copied.

2 Copy the text into
the clipboard using the
COPY command in the
EDIT menu (or the key
combination [Ctrl] + [C]).

3 Click the
place in the
text where
you wish to
paste the
copied text.

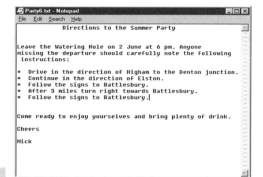

4 In the EDIT menu choose the command
PASTE or use the key combination [Ctrl] + [V].

145

The editor pastes the text from the **clipboard** at the current position of the insertion point. During the *copying* operation the previously selected section of text is retained.

Saving and loading texts

An advantage of using a computer compared with, for example, a typewriter lies in the possibility of saving the text you have written in a file. You then have the option of loading this text at a later time, looking at it again, printing it and, if necessary, amending it.

 In the FILE menu, choose the command SAVE.

If the text is new, the editor will open the dialog box *Save As*.

In this dialog box you can
see the text files that are
already saved in the folder
currently selected (called
the active folder). The folder
name is displayed in the list
box *Save in*.

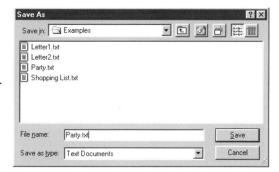

Would you like to change the folder?

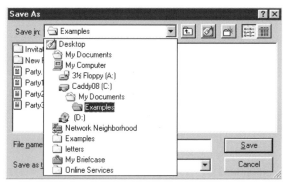

2 Open the list box
Save in.

3 Select the drive and folder
you want.

If necessary, refer back to Chapter 3 which shows how a folder can be
changed.

147

Do you want to create a new folder before saving the file?

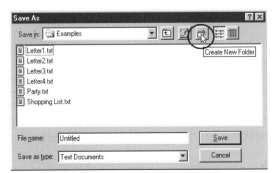

4 Click in the dialog box on the *Create New Folder* button.

5 Enter the folder name.

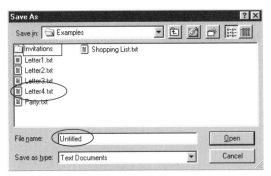

Here a new folder has been created in the dialog box.

6 Now enter the name of the new file in the *Filename* field.

7 Click on the *Save* button.

The editor will now display a file with the specified name and the filename extension *.txt* in the selected folder. You can now exit the editor and load this file again later.

In the *Filename* box, you just need to enter the name of the file. The editor will add the *.txt* extension automatically. When you see a file with this extension, you know that it can be edited with the Windows editor. Of course, Windows can be set up so that the filename extension does not appear (via the FOLDER OPTIONS command in the VIEW menu of the Explorer window). This is done under the *View* tab by clicking the check box to select "Hide file extensions for known file types".

If you have already saved the text previously in a file, save changes by simply choosing the SAVE command in the FILE menu. The *Save As* dialog box no longer appears since the editor already knows the filename. If you want to save the text under a new filename, choose the command SAVE AS in the FILE menu.

You will often come across text files in Windows. These may be, for example, files you have created in the editor. Other text files are supplied with Windows or other programs. Such files usually have the extension *.txt*. You can **load these files in the editor**, display them and, if necessary, print them out.

1 Start the Windows editor via the commands PROGRAMS / ACCESSORIES / EDITOR in the Start menu.

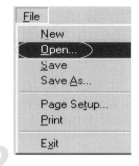

2 In the editor window choose the command OPEN in the FILE menu.

149

Windows will now display the *Open* dialog box. Via the *View Desktop* button you can call up the desktop folder shown opposite.

3 Now search for the folder with the text files by double-clicking on the icons displayed for *My Computer*, the drives and folders.

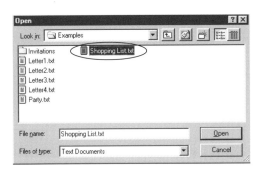

The window opposite shows a folder with several text files.

4 Click on the name of the text file to be opened.

5 Click on the *Open* button.

Windows will now open the selected file and display its contents.

The Windows editor can, however, only open fairly small text files (up 64 Kb). If the file is too big, you will be asked whether you want to open it in *WordPad*, a program described below.

Unfortunately, there are some text files which do not have the *.txt* extension, but *.ini*, *.bat* or *.log* instead. For these files to appear in the *Open* dialog box, you have to choose the entry *All Files (*.*)* in the *Files of type* drop-down list box. You will then be able to open these files as if they were text files.

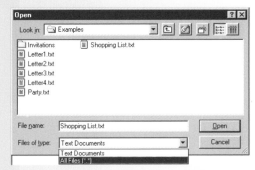

Searching text

Do you want to change something in a text several pages long? It might be, for example, that a particular word is to be replaced by another one. Or you might be looking for a specific passage. Of course you could read the text sentence by sentence to find the term in question. Experience shows, however, that it is very easy to miss something. From now on leave such tasks to Windows.

1 Load the text in the editor.

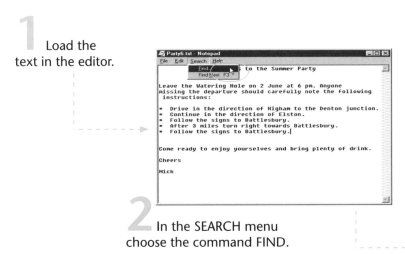

2 In the SEARCH menu choose the command FIND.

151

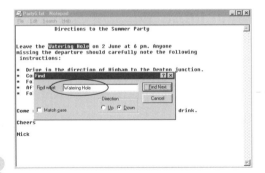

3 Enter the required term in the *Find what* field of the *Find* dialog box.

4 If necessary, click on the search direction options (*Up* or *Down*) and on *Match case* (capital or small letters).

5 Click on the *Find Next* button.

Terms that are found are highlighted in colour in the text. You can now close the *Find* dialog box and edit the text.

6 If you want to search for more instances of the term, choose the command FIND NEXT in the SEARCH menu or simply press Function key [F3].

If the term is not found, the editor indicates this in a message box.

7 Close the message box by clicking on the *OK* button.

Printing texts with the editor

There is still the question of how to print a loaded text file.

1 Make sure that the printer is turned on and online. Also check if there is enough paper.

2 In the FILE menu choose the command PRINT.

During printing the editor shows a small message box which tells you how the print operation is progressing, though the window will very soon disappear for short texts.

Creating documents with WordPad

Using the Windows editor, you can enter simple text and save it to a file for printing. However, many documents today are formatted more elaborately. Headings are emphasised in bold or the text may contain letters of different sizes. Windows has a program called WordPad for creating these sorts of documents.

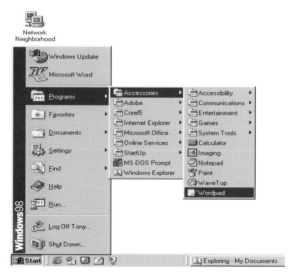

1 In the Start menu click on PROGRAMS / ACCESSORIES / WORDPAD.

Windows will now start the associated program with the name *Wordpad.exe*.

When activated, the window of the WordPad program is still empty and contains elements that you are already familiar with from other windows, such as title bar, menu bar, toolbar and status bar. Like the Windows editor, there is also a text area with an insertion point. Inside the text area the mouse pointer assumes the form of a text cursor.

Here is the empty WordPad window. In contrast to the Windows editor, this window has two toolbars, a status bar and a ruler bar.

Maybe your WordPad is not showing any toolbars or the ruler is missing? In the VIEW menu, you will find commands for toggling these elements on and off. (You have already met this kind of thing in Chapter 3 for folder windows. As you can see, there is a lot of similarity throughout Windows.)

To create a new document only two steps are necessary:

1 Click on the ☐ button (or choose the command NEW in the FILE menu).

2 Enter the text.

The window opposite contains the Directions to the Summer Party.

When entering text, proceed as already described in the previous lessons for the editor (the differences will be dealt with below).

You can use the same keys and functions for moving the insertion point, entering text, selecting and editing.

Also the functions for cutting, copying and pasting selected text areas can be used as in the Windows editor. However, in WordPad it's even simpler as you can use the buttons for these functions on the toolbar.

 Use this button to cut a selected text area from the WordPad window and paste it onto the clipboard.

 Use this button if the selected text is to remain and you need to copy it to the clipboard.

 Clicking on this button will paste the contents of the clipboard at the position of the insertion point in the text. This may be the text you previously cut or copied; but you can also select pictures or objects (i.e. sound files) in other programs, transfer them to the clipboard and paste them in.

 These buttons should already be familiar to you from Chapter 3 where they were used for copying files.

As promised, we shall now tell you about the differences of which you should take careful note. First of all, don't indent individual lines; you will learn a smarter way of doing this below.

There is another peculiarity that should be mentioned here. Often at the end of a line, the ⏎ key is pressed to start a new line. This is also called a **hard return** (on typewriters it is known as a carriage return). Even if you are familiar with this from the typewriter, you should refrain from pressing the ⏎ key when using WordPad on reaching the right-hand margin. Simply continue typing the text. WordPad has a function which detects the end of a line and automatically places the next word at the start of the next line. This is also called **wordwrap** and keeps text together within **paragraphs**.

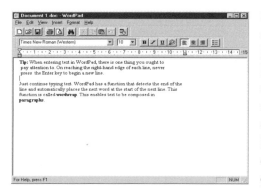

In the initial lines of the text opposite, the ⏎ key has been pressed at the end of the line. The lower lines, on the other hand, have been typed continuously: only at the end of the paragraph is there a hard break. Can you see the difference? Perhaps not. Why go to all this trouble then?

The advantages become apparent as soon as the line width in the document has to be changed. We have done this in the illustration below.

On reducing the line width the initial lines of the document appear rather mutilated. This is due to the **hard returns** inserted with the ⏎ key.

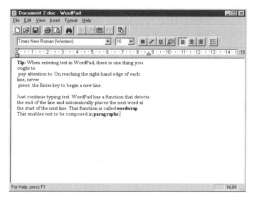

WordPad is forced to introduce a new line at the places concerned. To make the amended text look better you will now have to go back and edit the hard returns.

The lower part of the text, on the other hand, consists of one **paragraph**, and WordPad is able to adjust the lines automatically to the line width. You don't need to worry about this adjustment.

Formatting a text document

WHAT'S THIS?

Laying out a text document with various styles such as boldface, colour or larger size letters is also called **formatting**.

You will probably have already come across an invitation or letter that has been nicely formatted with certain passages printed in boldface or centred headings. In WordPad you can also **format** your documents in this way.

1 Click on the first line of the text.

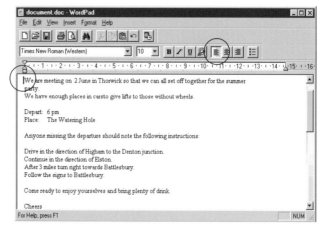

2 Click in the toolbar on the *Centre* button.

WordPad centres the first line.

Using the three buttons *Align Left, Centre* and *Align Right* you can align the text to the left margin, the centre of the line and to the right margin of the page respectively.

 The *Align Left* button ensures that lines are aligned to the left margin. When the text reaches the right-hand margin, the next word will be automatically transferred (wrapped) to the following line. Because the lines are of varying length at the right-hand margin, this is also known as a ragged margin. Left alignment is the normal form of text layout.

 Use the *Centre* button to centre text between the left and right margins. This arrangement is suitable for formatting headings, for example.

 The *Align Right* button causes lines of text to end at the right margin of the page, with the ragged margin occurring on the left. Unless you are composing Hebrew or Arabic, this button is unlikely to be used much.

Alignment relates to the **selected text area** or the current **paragraph**. If you press the ⏎ button at the end of a line when entering text, WordPad creates each line as a new paragraph. Alignment will then take a lot of effort. Again you can see that when entering text it pays to keep the text in paragraphs.

We shall now emphasise the heading with boldface and slightly larger letters.

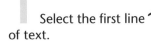 Select the first line of text.

159

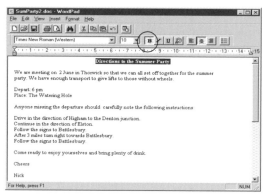

2 Click the *Bold* button.

The text will now be displayed in boldface.

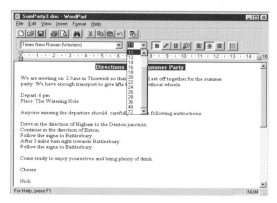

3 Click the *Font Size* drop-down list box.

4 Set a 14-point font size.

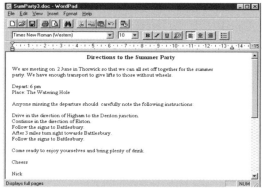

5 Click anywhere near the text to cancel the selection.

The document is now already looking better.

Various specialist terms are used in text formatting. The size of characters is not called character size or character height; the correct technical expression is **font size**. The numbers specify the font size in **points**, which is a unit like millimetres. The presentation of text uses so-called **fonts**. There are various fonts (Times Roman, Courier, Helvetica etc.) which are equivalent to different styles. You probably already know that the font in a newspaper looks very different from that of an advertising poster at your foodstore. And perhaps you remember the lettering on "wanted" posters in old Westerns that were laid out in a special font. (Note for youngsters: take a look at the leather label on your jeans. The logo of a well-known cola manufacturer also has a striking font.)

Besides font size and font style, you can also highlight passages in bold, italics or underline. WordPad provides three buttons for doing this:

B This button formats the selected text with **bold** letters.

I Clicking this button will cause the selected text to appear with sloping letters. This is also known as formatting in *italic* style.

To <u>underline</u> selected text, click this button.

In the Directions to the Summer Party created with the editor at the start of this chapter, various lines were highlighted with asterisks at the beginning of the line. Paragraphs emphasised like this are also called **bulleted lists**. Such a list can be formatted mush more elegantly in WordPad.

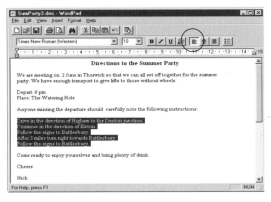

1 Select the lines or paragraphs that are to appear as a bulleted list.

2 Click in the toolbar on the *Bullets* button.

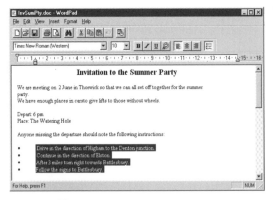

WordPad will now place a small dot (also called a bullet point or bullet) in front of the first line of the relevant paragraphs.

Where a paragraph consists of several lines, continuation lines are aligned to the start of the first line. We also say that the continuation lines are **indented** to the same **column** as the first line.

In the next step we shall emphasise the time and place of departure in bold and indent them. How to highlight in boldface has already been explained in the previous pages.

It could perhaps look like this:

Depart: 6pm
Place: The Watering Hole

More difficult is the indentation of the two texts written in normal (regular) style. Have you tried this out with the ⤶ key?

Depart: 6pm
Place: The Watering Hole

Here you can see that the result is not very convincing.

Depending on the length of a word, the tab positions for the individual lines do not match: on some lines you will have to insert two tab characters in order to position the indented words exactly under each other in the same column.

WordPad fixes the tab positions automatically like many other word processing programs. Nevertheless, you do have the option of setting tab positions manually to your requirements.

1 Select the lines or paragraphs for which the tabs are to be set.

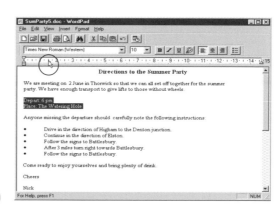

2 Left-click with the mouse at the position in the ruler where the tab is to appear.

163

WordPad marks the tab position with a little right-angle. At the same time the tab characters are inserted at this position in the selected text.

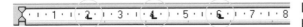

In this figure, three tabs have been positioned at 2, 4 and 6cm.

If necessary, these tab positions can be moved or deleted.

1 Point to a tab mark with the mouse.

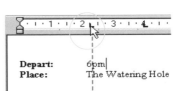

| Depart: | 6pm |
| Place: | The Watering Hole |

2 Move the mark to the left or right by dragging with the mouse.

A short broken line indicates the tab position in the text.

3 To delete a tab mark, drag it into the text area and then release the mouse button.

A further option for formatting a text document is provided by the **line length** for a text. WordPad begins a line at the left margin and ensures that the text is continued onto the next line. But how does WordPad know where the right and left margins for a line are?

 In the ruler bar you will see little triangles at the left and right margins.

These triangles are also called **indent markers**. You can specify the start and end of a line by means of the bottom left and bottom right indent markers. The top left indent marker defines the start of the first line for paragraphs with several lines. We say that this indent marker specifies the **first-line indent** (i.e. the indent of the first line of a paragraph). This will now be used to emphasise a paragraph in the text.

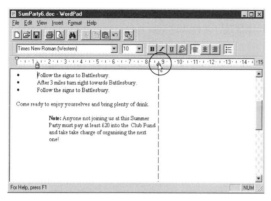

1 Point to the right indent marker and drag it to the left.

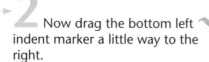

2 Now drag the bottom left indent marker a little way to the right.

This will cause the line width to be reduced. WordPad correspondingly indents the text and also takes care of the wordwrap. As a result you get a narrower paragraph text. In this way you can, for example, define the left and right indents of the text.

165

Saving, loading and printing documents in WordPad

In WordPad you can save text in files. They are given a name which you choose and also the file extension *.doc*. Saving works the same way as in the Windows editor which means you can use the SAVE command in the FILE menu. However, since WordPad has a toolbar, saving is even easier:

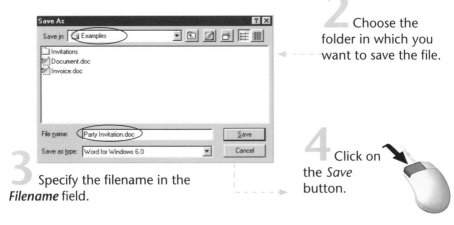

Click in the toolbar on the *Save* button.

In the case of a new document, the dialog box *Save As* appears.

Choose the folder in which you want to save the file.

Specify the filename in the *Filename* field.

Click on the *Save* button.

WordPad will now create the file and store the text.

You do not need to enter the extension *.doc* for the document. So long as the *Word for Windows 6.0* entry is chosen in the *Save as type* box, WordPad will use the extension *.doc*. You can also read and edit these text files with the Windows program *Word for Windows*; this is a word processing program which is considerably more powerful than WordPad and is frequently used in offices.

In the *Save as type* box you will find more file formats for saving text. For example, if you choose the type *.txt*, WordPad will save the document as a simple text file. You can load this type of file using the Windows editor. However, you will lose all your formatting when saving in a *.txt* file.

If you want to save a document that you have changed and which already has a filename, all you need to do is click *Save*. WordPad will then save the changes without further enquiry about the associated file. To save a document under a new name, choose the command SAVE AS in the FILE menu. The *Save As* dialog box shown above will then appear and you will be able to enter a new filename.

Text documents can be **loaded** in WordPad and then displayed, edited and printed.

1 Click in the WordPad window on the button shown opposite.

WordPad will now open this dialog box.

2 Select the folder containing the file to be loaded.

3 Click on the file you want to open.

4 Click the *Open* button.

167

WordPad now loads the file and displays the result in the document window. If the document has been formatted, the formatting will be shown on the screen.

Printing a **document** is even easier in WordPad than it is in the Windows editor.

 1 Click in the toolbar on the button shown opposite.

 During printing, WordPad will show this dialog box: it informs you how many pages have already been printed.

To cancel printing, click on the *Cancel* button.

Perhaps you have composed a multi-page document and would like to print just a few pages?

1 In the FILE menu, choose the command PRINT or press the key combination $Ctrl$ + V.

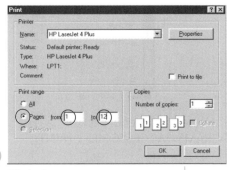

2 Click the *Pages* radio button.

3 Enter the page
numbers to be printed in
the *from* and *to* fields. - - - - - - → **4** Click the OK
button.

Do you just want to see how the document looks in the printout? Then
simply click the *Print Preview* button. WordPad then displays the
document in a reduced-size preview window.

WordPad provides further functions which we shall not go into here. Further
information on these can be found in WordPad Help.

Creating pictures with Paint

Windows contains the program Paint. Using this program you can edit
pictures and create small drawings.

1 In the Start menu, click on
PROGRAMS / ACCESSORIES / PAINT.

Windows will now start the program Paint which displays a window
containing a title bar and menu bar. These two elements will already
be familiar to you from other windows.

169

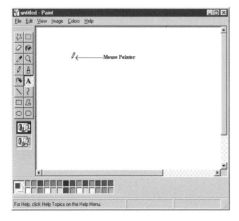

The **canvas** or drawing area is probably a new feature for you. If the mouse pointer is in this area it will take the form of a pencil or brush.

Along the left border of the window you will find a **toolbox** with buttons for the drawing functions. Along the bottom of the window is a **colour box** for selecting drawing colours.

 Using the pencil or brush whilst holding down the mouse button, you can draw lines (also called **free-form lines**) in the colour of your choice. With the brush you can also choose the line thickness.

To draw, carry out the following steps:

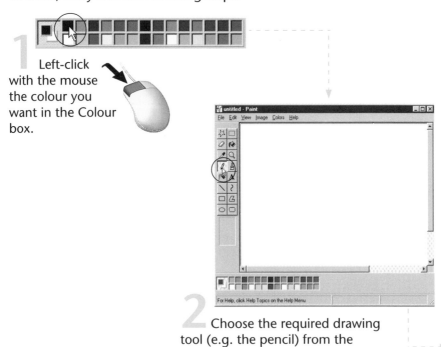

Left-click with the mouse the colour you want in the Colour box.

Choose the required drawing tool (e.g. the pencil) from the toolbox.

3 Click in the canvas.

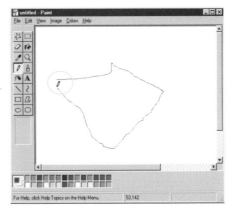

4 Drag the mouse across the canvas, keeping the left button pressed.

5 Release the mouse button.

6 Now click the brush as the tool to use.

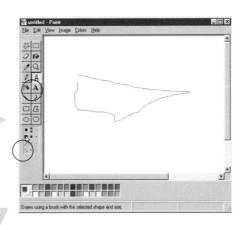

7 Specify the brush thickness in the field beneath the toolbox.

171

8 Drag the brush across the canvas, keeping the left mouse button depressed.

Depending on the tool chosen, a free-form line will be 'drawn' on the canvas in the chosen colour and line thickness.

The box for **choosing line thickness** is also displayed in the case of other tools (eraser, airbrush, etc.). By clicking on an option, the "thickness" of the tool can be changed.

Did you make a **mistake when drawing**? Press the key combination Ctrl + Z to **undo** the last drawing **command**. Using this key combination, you can, for example, remove the last line drawn. In Paint, the last three commands executed can be undone.

Unfortunately Paint does not have a function for deleting an element in a picture by clicking on it. However, there is a facility for erasing parts of the drawing using the eraser.

 1 Click on the eraser in the toolbox.

2 If required, choose another thickness for the eraser (this works in the same way as changing brush thickness).

3 Point to a place in the drawing.

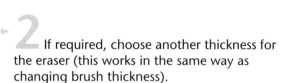

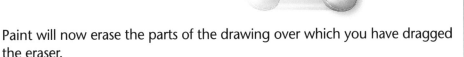

4 Hold down the left mouse button and drag the eraser across the drawing.

Paint will now erase the parts of the drawing over which you have dragged the eraser.

Normally you will work on a white background. However, you can **right-click** on a colour in the colour box. This colour is then used as the **background colour**. (The background colour fills a cleared area, the inside of enclosed shapes and forms the background to text frames.) Now right-click anywhere in the canvas and choose SELECT ALL, followed by CLEAR SELECTION in the context menu; Paint discards the current drawing and creates a new canvas with the chosen background. During "erasing", the tool also uses the chosen background colour. If you do this accidentally, choose another background colour.

The Paint program also offers further drawing tools by means of which you can produce special objects or achieve special effects.

 The *airbrush* can, for example, be used like the paint brush, but it produces a spray effect.

1 Click on the *airbrush* tool.

173

2 With the left mouse button held down, drag the tool across the canvas.

This will produce the airbrush effect. Dragging the tool more slowly will apply the colour more densely. The tool sprays with the most recently set colour.

Incidentally, the width of the drawing tool is set, similar to the brush, by means of the field shown opposite (located beneath the toolbox).

These buttons are for selecting tools to draw straight lines, curves, rectangles and other shapes.

Drawing lines and shapes (also called "figures") works in a similar way to most other tools.

1 Click on the tool required (in this case the rectangle).

2 Point to the start of the rectangle.

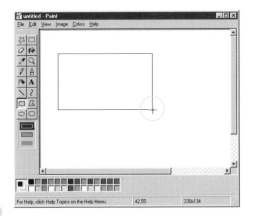

 Hold down the left mouse button and drag the mouse to the end of the figure.

As you drag, Paint draws the outline of the line or figure. As soon as you release the mouse button, Paint draws the figure or line to the size you choose.

By the way, for areas (e.g. rectangles, circles) you can use the options shown opposite to choose whether the figure will consist of a line in the foreground colour, be filled in by the background colour with a border or filled in by the foreground colour with no border.

The *polygon* tool can be used to draw complicated shapes by joining a number of lines end to end. To do this you have to "drag" the lines with the mouse, starting at the point of origin.

 Choose the *polygon* tool.

Point to the origin of the figure.

175

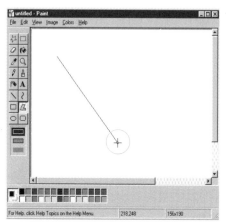

3 Holding the mouse button down, drag to the end of the first line.

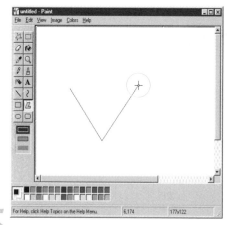

4 Click on the end to fix the line.

5 Repeat steps 3 and 4 to drag the following lines of the polygon.

Paint will automatically join the lines together.

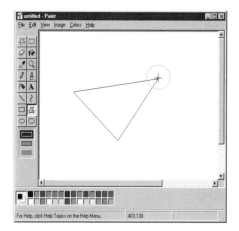

6 To close the polygon,
double-click on the end of the last line.

The tool automatically joins the ends of the lines together. If you double-click on the last point, the drawing function will automatically close the polygon with a line.

 Closed **figures** can be **filled** with the *Fill With Colour* tool.

1 Specify the desired fill colour by means of the colour box.

2 Select the *Fill With Colour* tool.

After you have selected the tool, Paint displays a paint-pot as the mouse pointer. As soon as you click on a figure its contents are filled with colour.

177

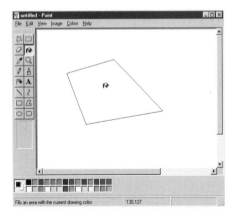

 Click on the
figure to be filled.

Drawings often have to be **labelled**. This is no problem using the *text* tool.

 Choose the
text tool.

2 Specify the text colour
by clicking in the colour box
with the mouse.

3 Point to the start of the text with
the mouse and drag the mouse diagonally down. Paint displays a rectangle
with blue broken lines.

4 Release the mouse button and type in the text you want.

5 Click anywhere near the text box.

Step 5 fixes the text at the current position in the drawing. You can no longer edit the text as this now effectively becomes a "picture" in the drawing. However, you have the option of removing the text with the eraser.

When entering text, the *Fonts* toolbar opposite appears.
Text can be formatted by

means of this toolbar. From the toolbar, you can choose the *font*, *size* and *formatting* for *bold*, *italic* and *underline*. Unlike WordPad though, the formatting applies to the whole text which is currently being written.

Using the *pick colour* tool (an eye-dropper) you can choose the foreground and background colours directly in the drawing (instead of in the colour box). You only have to click on the colours you want with the left and right mouse buttons respectively.

179

By choosing the *magnifier* tool you can zoom in on a section of the picture with a click of the left mouse button; a right click on the other hand will zoom out again.

Cutting out and copying parts of a picture

In the Windows editor and in WordPad you met the functions for selecting, cutting, copying and pasting. There are also similar options in Paint. Using these functions you can cut out parts of a picture from the drawing or copy them into the clipboard. The clipboard contents can then be pasted in the drawing as well as in other Windows programs (such as WordPad). Here you see a simple drawing which goes with the route directions to the summer party which we composed with WordPad. In the bottom left corner of the drawing are some models of direction arrows. We shall now paste a copy of the downward pointing arrow into part of the drawing. First of all, you have to select the part of the drawing you want to edit.

 1 First choose the *select* tool.

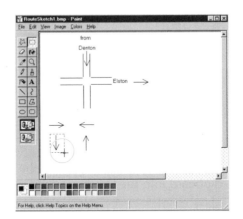

2 Point with the mouse in the top left corner of the area to be cut out.

3 Hold down the left mouse button and drag the mouse diagonally across the area.

Paint selects the area using a rectangle with broken lines. As soon as you release the left mouse button, this rectangle is fixed as a selection. Now you can cut out this area, copy it and then paste it from the clipboard.

These three functions can be initiated via the EDIT menu or by using the following key combinations:

Ctrl + X   Cuts out the selected area and copies it to the clipboard. The selected area vanishes and is replaced by the background colour.

Ctrl + C   Copies the selected area to the clipboard. This does not alter the drawing.

Ctrl + V   The contents of the clipboard are pasted into the top left corner of the area of the drawing as a selection. You can drag this selected area with the mouse to any position you want in the drawing.

You have already met these key combinations. Windows uses them in all programs to cut out, copy and paste selected areas.

1   Now press the key combination Ctrl + C to copy the selected area of the picture onto the clipboard.

2   Next press the key combination Ctrl + V to paste the contents of the clipboard into the window again.

3   Point in the top left corner to the selected area containing the pasted picture.

181

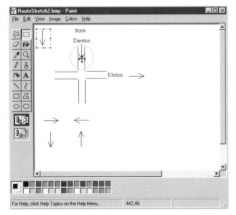

4 Holding down the left mouse button, drag the selected part to the desired position in the drawing.

5 Click on any point outside the selection.

Perhaps you have already noticed in the last step that to move part of a drawing, you only have to select it and then move the selected area in the drawing by using the mouse.

The last step cancels the selection and pastes the part of the picture into the drawing.

Saving, loading and printing in Paint

The functions described in the previous pages can be used to edit drawings, invitations and pictures in Paint.

As soon as the picture or drawing is ready, it can be saved in a file. This works in Paint in the same way as in other programs.

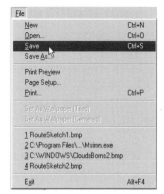

1 In the FILE menu, choose the command SAVE or press the key combination *Ctrl* + *S*.

2 In the *Save As* dialog box specify the drive and folder where the file is to be stored.

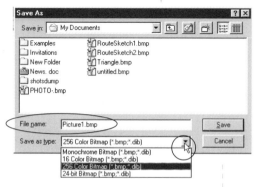

3 Type the filename in the *Filename* field.

183

4 If necessary, you can still drop down the *Save as type* list box to choose the number of colours in which to save the picture.

5 Click the *Save* button to save the picture in the file.

Paint creates a new file and saves the picture in it. Of course the dialog box *Save As* only appears the first time you save a new picture. If the file already exists, the SAVE command in Paint will save any changes without further enquiry. To specify another filename you will have to choose the command SAVE AS in the FILE menu.

Pictures saved as a *.bmp* file type can be **loaded** in Paint. These might be pictures or drawings you have created yourself. In addition, you can also load and edit *.bmp*-pictures from other sources in Paint. For example, there are a number of *.bmp*-files supplied with Windows and many CD-ROMs also have *.bmp*-pictures.

1 Start the *Paint* program.

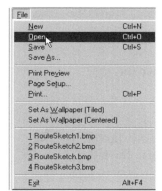

2 In the FILE menu, choose the command OPEN.

Alternatively you can also use the key combination Ctrl + O to activate the OPEN command.

3 In the dialog box *OPEN* select the folder with the files.

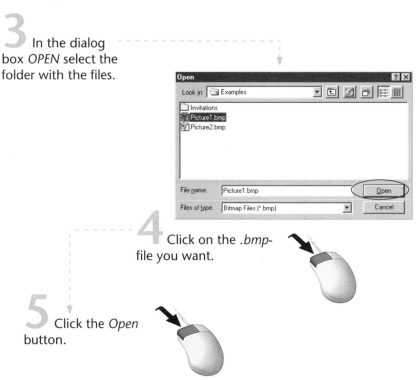

4 Click on the *.bmp*-file you want.

5 Click the *Open* button.

Paint opens the *.bmp*-file required and
loads the picture contained in this file.
You can now edit, save and/or print
the picture.

You can load **pictures** in Paint and then **output them on a printer**.
Depending on the printer used, Windows will convert coloured pictures
into a black and white representation if necessary.

1 Start the
program Paint.

2 Load the file that has
the picture you want.

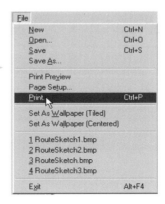

3 In the menu FILE, choose the command
PRINT. Alternatively you can also press the key
combination $\boxed{Ctrl}+\boxed{P}$.

Paint now opens the *Print* dialog box for the selection of print options.

4 Click the *OK* button.

Paint now starts to print out the picture. Even if the whole of the picture is not visible in the window, the complete picture will be output on the printer.

Creating a background picture for Windows

Windows can display backgound pictures on the desktop (see Chapter 11). These background pictures must be saved as *.bmp*-files. This means, however, that you can edit and/or create them using Paint. For example, after installation, the Windows folder should contain the file *Clouds.bmp*. Below we show by means of an example how in Paint such a picture can be loaded, modified and then used as a desktop background.

1 Start the program Paint.

2 In the FILE menu, choose the command OPEN.

187

3 Load the file *Clouds.bmp* that is in the Windows folder.

4 Modify the picture to fit in with your ideas. For example, you could insert a text into the picture.

5 Save the picture in the *Windows* folder on the hard disk.

You will now be able to reload the picture later on and edit it. When you have finished the picture for the desktop-background, Windows will have to be "informed". A picture can be displayed on the desktop or used to fill in the background. This will be considered when we select the following options.

1 In the FILE menu choose the command SET AS WALLPAPER (TILED) if you want the complete background to be filled.

2 If you want to display the picture in its present size, choose SET AS WALLPAPER (CENTRED).

3 Close the program Paint.

The command SET AS WALLPAPER (CENTRED) is to be preferred. The option TILED fills the entire desktop background. If the picture is smaller than the desktop, it will be output as multiple tiles placed next to one another.

Here you see the new desktop background where the picture has been placed in the centre. In Chapter 11 we will demonstrate how to remove this background picture.

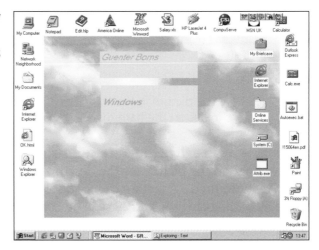

189

Text with pictures and other objects

In this chapter you have learnt how to create a text in WordPad and a picture in Paint. Now it's time to use the power of Windows. How about including the route sketch in the text for the Directions to the Summer Party? Then only the text document will have to be printed and the sketch will automatically be output with it. Does your computer have a sound card? If so, you can provide your text with sound documents that can be selected with a mouse click (working with sound is dealt with in Chapter 7).

Transferring a picture into text is quite simple - in fact you already know how to do it. You know how to select parts of documents in WordPad or Paint, copy them onto the clipboard and paste them somewhere else in the document area. For most programs, Windows supports the transfer of data from another program via the clipboard.

1 Start the WordPad program and load the file containing the text for the Directions.

2 Insert a blank line after the route Directions.

This is where we shall put the sketch.

3 Start the
program Paint, and
load the picture with
the route sketch.

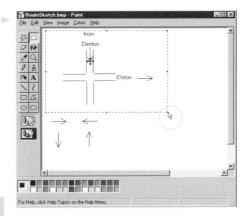

4 Select the part of the sketch
to be transferred.

5 Using the key combination
⌘ + ⒞, copy the selected part onto
the clipboard.

6 Change to the WordPad
window and click on the place
where the picture is to be inserted.

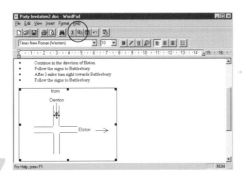

7 Paste the picture from the clipboard into the
text. You can use either the *Paste* button or the key
combination ⌘ + ⒱.

191

The text document now contains the picture. As usual, you can save, print or revise the text document. To delete the picture again, you will have to select the area and then use the ⌊ *Delete* ⌋ key.

WordPad also lets you include in a text document files prepared using other programs. These files may contain texts, pictures, sounds or other data. Thus, these files are called **objects**. To incorporate an object file in a text document, proceed as follows:

1 Start WordPad and create the document with text.

2 Position the insertion point at the place in the text where the object data is to be inserted.

3 In the INSERT menu choose the command OBJECT.

4 In the dialog box *Insert Object* select the option "Create from File".

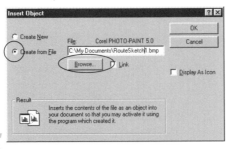

5 Click the *Browse* button.

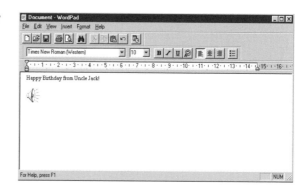

6 Choose the folder and then the file with the object data. In this case we chose to insert a sound file.

7 Close any dialog boxes that are open.

The inserted object is now displayed in the WordPad document. Here you see the icon for a sound document. On selecting the icon with a double-click, the object will be opened. In this example you will then hear the sound document.

193

Quick progress check

Having gone through this chapter you will already know almost everything that there is to know about Windows. It might be a good idea to check your knowledge and newly learned skills with the aid of the following exercises. After each exercise we give the lesson where the answer can be found.

➡ **Create a text with the Windows editor and save it in a .txt-file on a diskette.**

(You will find the answer in Chapter 4 in the Lessons "Creating texts with the editor" and "Saving and loading texts")

➡ **See which text files are supplied with Windows and load them.**

(The files will be found in the Windows folder. You will see how a *.txt*-file is displayed in Chapter 4 in the Lesson "Saving and loading texts")

➡ **Create an invitation using the program WordPad.**

(Answers in Chapter 4 in the Lesson "Creating documents with WordPad")

➡ **Create a picture of your own for the desktop background.**

(Answer in Chapter 4 in the Lesson "Creating a background picture for Windows")

➡ **Create a text and insert different objects in it.**

(Answer in Chapter 4 in the Lesson "Text with pictures and other objects")

In the next chapter you will learn how to deal with documents in an even smarter way.

What's in this chapter?

You already know how to start a program and load a document. But there are smarter ways of working with documents in Windows. You are going to learn how to recall the last 15 documents you worked on. In addition, you will find out how a document can be opened directly in Explorer or in the *My Computer* window. We shall also show how you can display the contents of a file without having to activate a program.

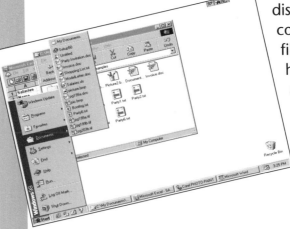

You already know about:

You are going to learn about:

How document files are represented

In Chapter 3 you learnt how files are displayed in the *My Computer* window (or its subfolder windows) and in the Explorer window. Now you have had a bit more experience in handling files, we shall go into the subject of managing documents a little more deeply.

In Chapter 3 it was explained that files have a name and a name extension and are also represented by an icon. The window opposite contains files together with their names and icons. Windows identifies the **type of file** from the filename extension.

Each program can only read files of a certain file type. For example, using WordPad you can read and edit files of file type *.txt*, *.doc*, and *.rtf*. But WordPad cannot process graphics files (even if you can paste a picture or a *.bmp*-file into a text). The Windows editor, on the other hand, only edits simple text files with the extension *.txt*. The same applies to Paint, which can only read graphics files with the extension *.bmp*. To edit a document file, you therefore need the program which was used to create this file or which can read the file type.

If you look at the document files in the above picture and compare the representation with that on your computer, you might notice one or two points:

➡ For one thing, Windows always uses a particular icon for a filename extension. All *.txt*-files are usually displayed with a little notepad icon; files with the extension *.doc* have a different icon; and so do graphics files with the extension *.bmp*.

➡ In Chapter 3 in the lesson "What are folders and files?" you will see a table listing the icons for some file types. However, in the above picture different icons have been used for files with the extensions *.bmp* and *.doc*.

Why is this so and what does it mean? The answers are really quite simple:

➡ When Windows is newly installed on a computer, the filename extensions and file icons for some document files are predefined. For example, Windows uses the program Paint for *.bmp*-files and *.doc*-files are edited using WordPad. As a result, Windows uses these programs to open the corresponding document files. At the same time, icons for these programs are used to represent the document files in Explorer and in folder windows.

➡ The majority of users will install additional programs under Windows. These might be word processing or spreadsheet programs; and some programs are used for creating and editing graphics and so on. If, for example, such a program supports a particular file type, the Windows settings are correspondingly modified. This will also have an effect on the icons that are displayed for document files.

You will therefore see file icons for the file various types that are determined by the programs installed on a particular computer.

 If, for example, you have Microsoft Word installed on your computer, the icon opposite will appear for *.doc*-files.

 If only the program Paint for editing *.bmp*-graphics is installed, then Windows will use the icon for files shown here.

199

In the display of the folder *Examples* on the previous pages, the icon shown here was used for *.bmp*-files. The computer concerned has a special program with the name *Paint Shop Pro* installed for editing graphics. All the file types supported by this program are assigned this icon.

If the icons for a particular data type are displayed differently on your computer, there is no need to worry: the computer simply has different programs installed for opening these particular documents. In the next lesson you will see how this affects the opening of documents.

Textfile.asc

How to open document files

You already know how to open a document file:

1 You start the program which was used to create the document concerned.

2 Open the FILE menu and choose the command OPEN.

3 In the *Open* dialog box, select the folder and then the document file you want.

4 Confirm your entry with the
Open button.

The particular document file will now be loaded into the program
window.

The method described here should work for all programs that conform
reasonably well to the rules established for Windows. You have already met
this procedure in Chapter 4 for different Windows programs. If a program has
a toolbar, the *Open* button can be used to load documents.

However, isn't this approach a bit long-winded? In the previous chapters
you learnt that programs can be opened by double-clicking the associated
file. But a folder window also displays the document files saved there.
Do you always have to know precisely whether a file is a program or a
document? Why shouldn't it be possible to open a document just by
double-clicking on the file icon?

In fact this approach works very well indeed:

1 Open the
window of the folder
where the document
files were saved.

2 Double-click on a
document file icon.

Windows starts the correct program for this file type and then automatically loads the selected document file. You will see the document immediately in the program window. Here, for example, a file with the *.txt* extension has been selected by double-clicking.

You can try this out for different file types. Provided Windows recognises the file type, the associated program will be started and the relevant document file loaded. It could hardly be simpler.

Creating documents on the desktop

Have you created a document that you will need to use frequently? This could, for example, be a model letter. So it would be particularly useful if the document concerned appeared as an icon on the desktop. A simple double-click is enough to open the program together with the document. How to create such a model will now be shown using a *.doc*-file as an example.

1 Start WordPad or a program that can create *.doc*-files.

2 Create the document that you want to use as a model.

3 Save the document as a file
in a folder.

4 Open the folder window where the
document is saved.

5 Select the document file with
a mouse click.

6 Hold the right mouse button down
and drag the document icon to a free
area on the desktop.

7 Release the mouse button.

Move Here
Copy Here
Create Shortcut(s) Here
Cancel

8 In the context menu, choose
the command CREATE SHORTCUT(S)
HERE.

Modelle.doc

9 If required, you can now
rename the shortcut.

Having created the shortcut, you only need to double-click the shortcut symbol on the desktop to open the document. You can now edit the document and, if necessary, save it under a new name.

Loading a document in different programs

Do you have several programs installed under Windows that support the same file type? This would be the case if, for example, you set up Microsoft Word on your PC. You can then open files with the extension .doc using both Word and the Windows program WordPad. The same applies, for example, to graphics programs which create .bmp-files.

You might now have a problem: double-clicking one of these files will often load the "wrong" program. Maybe you prefer to edit a .doc -file using WordPad (e.g. because you are more familiar with that program) although Microsoft Word is started when you double-click the file? Perhaps you find it too laborious to start Word first and then load the file? There is an easier way, however:

1 Open the folder window where the document file is saved.

2 **Select** the document file with a **single** mouse click.

3 Hold the ⏎ key down and **right-** click the selected file with the mouse.

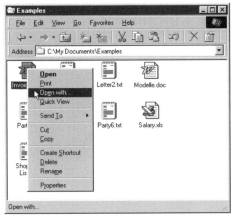

4 Click on the command OPEN WITH.

5 Use the scroll bar to search for the program you want to use to open the document file.

The trick in all this is to keep the ⏎ key held down when opening the context menu. Windows then shows two commands for opening files. The OPEN command in the context menu starts the standard program (similar to double-clicking the document file). On the other hand, via the command OPEN WITH in the dialog box of the same name, you can select the program you want for editing document files.

 Click the program name and then the *OK* button.

Windows starts the program you have chosen and then loads the document file.

TIP

If you double-click to select a file of a file type that Windows doesn't recognise, the *Open With* dialog box opens automatically. If you know what kind of data is in the file, you can select a program from the list. Click the check box "Always use this program to open this type of file" to delete the check mark. Only then should you close the dialog box via the *OK* button. If you forget to do this, Windows remembers the program activated last time and continues to use it for this file type. It is annoying if you activate a program which cannot be used to edit the file.

TIP

When you double-click a document file, do you want Windows to always open it with the program you prefer? If so, after selecting the program, select the check box "Always use this program to open this type of file" in the *Open With* dialog box. As soon as you close the dialog box by clicking the *OK* button, Windows will change the settings for this document type. The next time you double-click, the program you chose will be used. You can also use this tip if you inadvertently register the wrong program to open a document file in the *Open With* dialog box.

Quick viewing file contents

Have you met this situation before? You receive a diskette containing various document files. Now you open the window displaying the files and try and find out quickly what is in a particular file. Double-clicking a particular file is ruled out here for the following reasons:

➡ You don't want to edit the file anyway and loading the document into the application might take too long. If you want to look at three or four files, double-clicking would be time consuming.

➡ The program required for loading the document is not installed on your computer.

In the second case you've got a real problem. But (as so often) Windows provides a neat way out.

1 Select the file you are interested in by **left-clicking** with the mouse.

2 Now **right-click** the file.

If Windows recognises the file type, the command QUICK VIEW will appear.

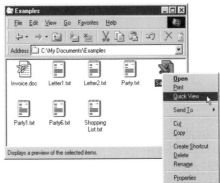

3 In the context menu click the command QUICK VIEW.

207

Windows opens the *Quick View* window
and displays the contents of the document
file concerned. For example, it could be an
Excel table as shown in the window
opposite.

The Windows QUICK VIEW function can
display the contents of many document
files without having to start the relevant
application. This allows you to rapidly see
the contents of various files.

For document files created with Microsoft Office 97,
Windows Quick View unfortunately shows only a
blank window. The reason is that although Windows
recognises the file type, the new Office format cannot
read it.

Opening the most recent documents list

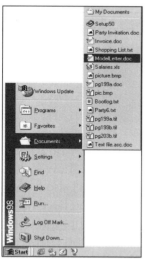

If you open a document file, Windows will
note its name. The last 15 documents you
have opened are summarised in a list that
you can look at and load via the Start
menu.

1 Open the Start menu
and point with the mouse to
the command DOCUMENTS.

2 Click on one of the document
names listed in the submenu.

Windows automatically loads the program associated with the document as well as the document itself.

If you want to **clear the list** of the 15 most recently **opened files,** carry out the following steps:

1 In the Start menu click on the command SETTINGS / TASKBAR & START MENU...

2 Activate the tab *Start Menu Programs.*

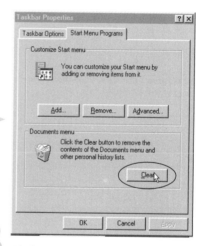

3 Click the *Clear* button in the "Documents menu".

4 Close the window via the OK button.

If you have worked through the previous chapters you will now know the most important functions of Windows. You will know how to start programs and how to work with folders and files. You will also know how documents are printed. If there is still something you have not quite mastered this is no problem. If you need to, read through the relevant passages in the chapters concerned. The following chapters will develop this knowledge (Chapter 6 for instance) and show what other interesting things can be done with Windows (as in Chapter 7). Chapters 8, 9, 10 and 11 deal with more specialised topics.

What's in this chapter?

In the previous chapters you have already seen how a document can be printed by means of a program. In this chapter you will learn to set up a printer under Windows and to create an icon for it on the desktop. Windows can place documents for printing into temporary storage. You can therefore continue working with a program before the document has finished printing. In the following you will see how to produce a summary of the documents being printed and how to pause a printout or cancel it altogether.

You already know about:

Working with programs and
windows   30, 50
Printing from programs   166, 183

You are going to learn about:

Setting up a new printer   212
Creating an icon for the printer on
the desktop   219
How to print   222
Changing printer settings   225
Managing printers   228

Setting up a new printer

Windows supports printers from various manufacturers which you can connect to your computer. However, before using a printer you will have to set it up. For this purpose Windows has a **printer driver** installed. This is a program that "intercepts" documents to be printed and prepares them for the printer. For installing a printer, Windows has a "Wizard" which guides you through the individual steps; it is activated via the *Printers* folder. This folder will be found in the *My Computer* window or in the Start menu. To set up a printer carry out the following steps. Files may be needed from the Windows 98 CD-ROM, so get it ready.

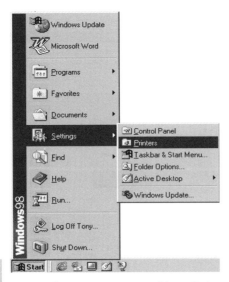

Open the Start menu and in the SETTINGS submenu choose the command PRINTERS.

Windows now opens the *Printers* window showing the icons of previously installed printers together with an additional icon called *Add Printer.*

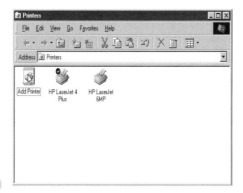

2 Double-click on the
Add Printer icon.

Windows now starts the
Wizard which guides you
through setting up the new
printer. You will encounter
such wizards quite often in
Windows. Their operation is
quite simple. The *Next* button
moves you through the
following pages of the Wizard.

If you realise at a particular
step that you have forgotten

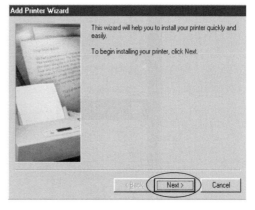

an input or you want to refer back to something, just click on *Back*. The
Wizard will then display the preceding page. We presume that you are
clear about using the *Cancel* button for cancelling the configuration of a
new printer and for exiting the Wizard. As soon as you see the start
page of the Wizard you can carry out the individual steps for setting up
the printer.

1 If the printer is only attached to your own computer, click the "Local Printer" option on this page.

For printers in a network, choose the second option (see Chapter 9).

2 Click the *Next* button.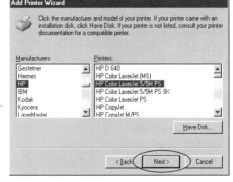

If your printer is not listed and you have a diskette from the printer manufacturer, you can install the printer by clicking the *Have Disk* button.
Windows opens a dialog box so you can choose a floppy disk drive. However, this situation is rare and so will not be dealt with in this book.

3 Choose the manufacturer of your printer from the left list box.

4 Next click on the printer model in the right list box.

5 Click the *Next* button.

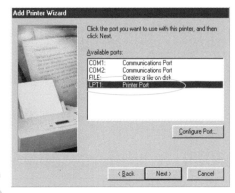

6 On this page choose the port via which the printer is connected to your computer.

Most printers are connected to what is called a **parallel interface** which is assigned the designation **LPT1:**.

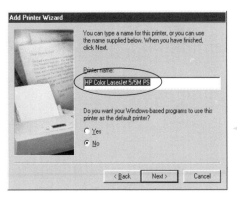

7 Click the *Next* button.

8 If necesssary, change the (default) name of the printer on this page.

9 Find out if the printer will be used for all Windows applications as the default printer.

10 Click the *Next* button.

Windows programs normally output data to the **default printer**, which can be specified in the top dialog box. This is the printer that is preset after program startup. Some systems have more than one printer attached. You can then choose what printer you want to use in any application by means of the *Printer* dialog box. So, for example, the output for a graphics program could be output on a colour printer whilst the word processor uses a laser printer as the default device.

This step completes the installation of the printer. Of course it is not guaranteed that all the settings will be correct. After setting up a printer driver, Windows can **output a test page**. If this appears correct, then it's all right for you to use the printer.

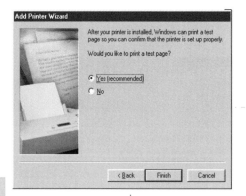

1 Choose whether to set the "Yes (recommended)" option to output a test page.

2 Click the Next button.

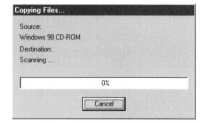

Windows will now copy the printer driver files onto your hard disk.

If this message box appears, Windows requires the installation CD-ROM.

1 First of all, insert the required CD-ROM (with the printer drivers) into the disk drive.

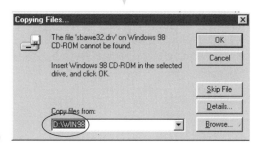

3 Click the *OK* button.

2 If this dialog box appears, enter in the *Source* field the name of the drive together with the path of the installation files.

On the Windows CD-ROM the printer drivers are in the folder \Win98. In the picture above, the CD-ROM has been inserted into the disk drive called D:. If you do not know what the CD-ROM drive is called, you can use the *Browse* button and search for the available drives and folders on the drive.

Did this message appear on your screen?

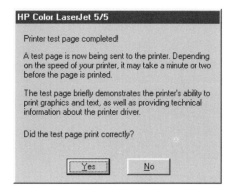

1 Check whether the test page was error-free.

2 Click the *Yes* button if everything is O.K. If there are problems, choose *No*.

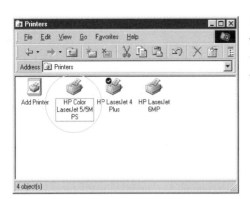

If everything went well, the icon for the new printer will appear in the *Printers* folder. You can then work with the printer.

Did you choose the *No* button in the message box above because there was something wrong with the printout? If so, Windows automatically opens the Help window shown opposite. By using the options and the *Next* button in this window, you will receive further information on the diagnosis and remedy of problems.

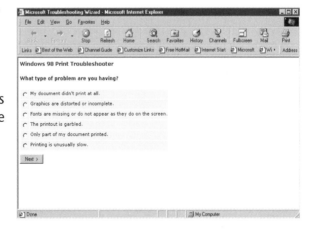

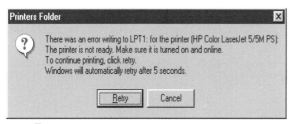

If, on the other hand, the *Printers folder* message box opposite appears, then there is a printer error only.

1 Check whether the printer is connected and turned on.

2 If necessary, put the printer *Online*.

3 Check whether the printer has enough paper.

As soon as the error has been cleared, Windows resumes printing. This message box also appears when printing a document if the printer has a malfunction. You should then check the printer.

Sometimes things go wrong when printing and you have to cancel the the printout after it's begun. It's then all right to turn off the printer and click the *Cancel* button in the message box. Windows then deletes all data not yet output.

Creating an icon for the printer on the desktop

In the following lessons you will see how Windows manages printouts and how printer settings can be changed. But to do this you must open the Print Manager window for the particular printer. Normally this means opening the *Printer* folder window and selecting the printer icon you want by double-clicking. It is therefore recommended to set up the printer icon on the desktop.

1 Open the Start menu and from the SETTINGS submenu choose the item PRINTER.

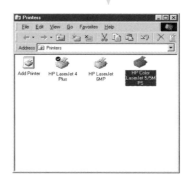

2 Drag the icon for the printer you want to a free area on the desktop whilst holding down the **right** mouse button.

3 Release the right mouse button.

4 In the context menu choose the command CREATE SHORTCUT(S) HERE.

5 If required, modify the name of the (shortcut) printer icon set up by Windows.

The icon for the printer you have just set up is now located on the desktop. You can now open the associated window, drag documents to the printer icon and print.

Do you want to locate the icon not only on the desktop but also in the Start menu or in the *Quick Launch* toolbar?

1 Holding down the left mouse button, drag the printer icon from the printer folder to the START button of the Start menu.

2 Release the mouse button.

The icon is now located in the Start menu.

To set up the printer icon in the Quick Launch toolbar, drag the icon to that position. As soon as you release the left mouse button, Windows creates a button for the printer.

How to print

Windows offers various options for printing. Unfortunately, different Windows applications behave in slightly different ways in this respect. Usually you will be printing from a program.

 1 If the program has a toolbar with a *Print* button, click this.

Generally, the application will print the current document in full without further enquiry. You met this facility in Chapter 4 with the program WordPad. If there is not a toolbar, then proceed as follows:

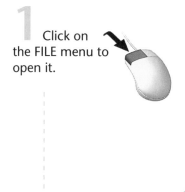

1 Click on the FILE menu to open it.

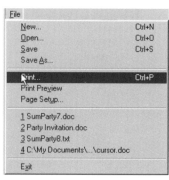

File	
New...	Ctrl+N
Open...	Ctrl+O
Save	Ctrl+S
Save As...	
Print...	Ctrl+P
Print Preview	
Page Setup...	
1 SumParty7.doc	
2 Party Invitation.doc	
3 SumParty8.txt	
4 C:\My Documents\...\cursor.doc	
Exit	

2 Click the command PRINT.

If the menu displays the key combination ⌈Ctrl⌉ + ⌈P⌉, you can also activate the print function directly using these buttons.

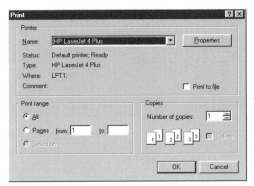

3 Set the **print options** you want.

4 Click *OK* to start the printout.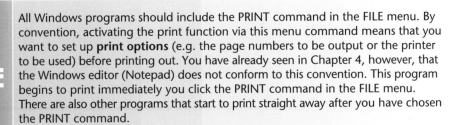

All Windows programs should include the PRINT command in the FILE menu. By convention, activating the print function via this menu command means that you want to set up **print options** (e.g. the page numbers to be output or the printer to be used) before printing out. You have already seen in Chapter 4, however, that the Windows editor (Notepad) does not conform to this convention. This program begins to print immediately you click the PRINT command in the FILE menu. There are also other programs that start to print straight away after you have chosen the PRINT command.

Chapter 5 dealt with managing documents. It also described how Windows recognises a file type by means of the file extension. Many documents can therefore be directly loaded in the associated program by double-clicking the file. For particularly urgent printouts Windows offers a similar and very smart way to print a document directly from a file.

1 Open the folder window containing the document file to be printed.

2 Select this file with a mouse click.

3 Right-click the selected file with the mouse.

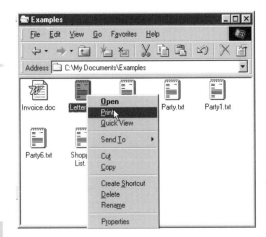

4 Left-click the command PRINT in the context menu.

Windows will now automatically open the document in the associated program and start the printout. As soon as the document has been printed, the program is exited without further action.

TIP

You can also use the mouse to drag a document file from a folder window to a printer icon. When the document icon is over the printer icon, release the left mouse button. This process is also called **drag-and-drop**. In most cases, Windows prints the document through the associated application. Only when Windows fails to recognise an application that can edit this type of document, does it report an error. Printing by drag-and-drop is especially smooth when the printer icon has been created as a shortcut on the desktop.

Changing printer settings

Do you want to print a page in landscape rather than in portrait orientation? Is the printer to fetch paper from the envelope tray? Do you have several printers and want to change the output device you are using? Windows offers various options for changing printer settings.

Have you opened the *Print* dialog box (see the previous lesson)?

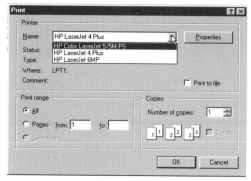

To change the printer, click the *Name* drop-down list box.

From the list select the name of the printer you want.

225

Now you can specify the options for this printer or for the current document and start the printout via the *OK* button.

When installing a new printer (see above), you will be asked if you want it to be set as the **default printer**. In the *Print* dialog box you will see that Windows can support several printers at the same time. A program can, however, only use one specific printer for printing out. The default printer is automatically used at program startup. Opening the *Print* dialog box displays this printer's name in the *Name* box. If you now choose another printer, this setting will remain for the **current session** of the program. If you exit the program and start again later, the default printer will be used again.

Unfortunately there is still a series of older Windows programs that can only use the default printer. If you choose another printer in the *Print* dialog box, it will automatically be set as the default printer. If necessary, you will then have to consider going back to this setting after printing.

In the *Print* dialog box you will see the *Properties* button. Via this button you can open the printer properties window showing various tabs (*Paper*, *Graphics* etc.).

Click *Properties* in the *Print* dialog box.

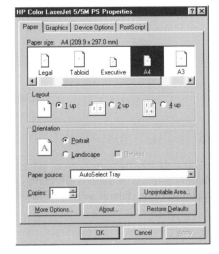

The picture opposite shows the Properties window for a printer.

The **number** of **tabs** and their **content** depends on the particular printer installed. However, the most important options are similar or identical for most printers.

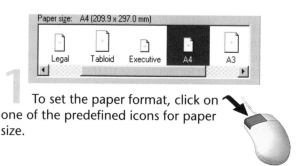

To set the paper format, click on one of the predefined icons for paper size.

Some printers even let you set customised paper formats.

If you want to print in landscape instead of portrait orientation, click on *Landscape*.

By means of the *Paper source* drop-down list box, you can choose which tray the printer can draw its paper from.

Via the *Restore Defaults* button, Windows resets the printer properties to the factory settings. If there is anything wrong with the printout, you can return again to these default settings and see if they work.

Managing printers

If, for example, you are printing a document several hundred pages long, it will be some time before the last sheet comes out of the printer. The program you used to print the document will, in most cases, have done its job after a few seconds. Therefore you do not want to be sitting around idly waiting until the printer has finished. Windows provides temporary storage for the print data on the hard disk and, if necessary, passes this data on to the printer in the background. We also say that the **printouts** are spooled as **print jobs** in the **print queue**.

 While there is still data to be printed out, a small printer icon appears next to the clock in the taskbar.

 If there is a **problem** with the **printout**, this is usually indicated by a question mark in the printer icon.

You will therefore always see what is going on with the printer and you can continue to work with the program. It is also possible to load other documents or even exit the program that was concerned with the printing. Many users make use of a number of programs at the same time or send several documents to the printer one after the other. How can you tell which documents are currently in the print queue? And how can a print job be paused or even cancelled?

For this you need to have the printer control window open (do not confuse this with the *Printers* folder window).

HP LaserJet 4
Plus

1 Double-click on the printer icon.

You can use the printer icon in the right corner of the taskbar or the printer icon in the *Printers* folder. If you have set up a printer icon as a shortcut on the desktop, choose this by double-clicking.

Windows now opens the window shown opposite.

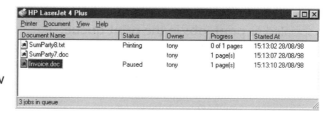

Document Name	Status	Owner	Progress	Started At
SumParty8.txt	Printing	tony	0 of 1 pages	15:13:02 28/08/98
SumParty7.doc		tony	1 page(s)	15:13:07 28/08/98
Invoice.doc	Paused	tony	1 page(s)	15:13:10 28/08/98

This window displays the contents of the **print queue** with the **print jobs**: that is those documents that have not yet finished printing. Each print job is displayed on a separate line with the job currently being printed appearing in the top line. The window has various columns of information:

➡ In the first column you can see the **document name**. This is allocated by the print program and usually corresponds with the document filename.

➡ The **Status** column gives information about the status of each of the print jobs. The top line with the document currently being printed contains, for example, a note of a current problem. For print jobs still waiting, you can see if these have been paused.

229

⟹ In a network, the **Owner** column tells you who wants to print this document. This is useful if, for example, there is a printer error. You can then inform the owner of the document.

⟹ In the case of multi-page documents you can see from the **Progress** column how many pages have already been printed.

⟹ The last column, **Started At**, gives the time when the document was passed by the program for printing.

You can use the menu bar to control the printed output and, for example, pause print jobs.

1 In the *Document Name* column, click on the print job you want.

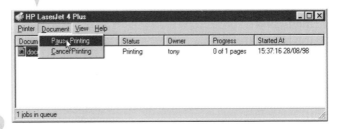

2 Open the DOCUMENT menu and choose the command PAUSE PRINTER.

In the *Status* column, the message "Paused" appears. Windows will now stop sending this print job to the printer until you release it again. This

allows you to place a very long document back in the print queue and give short-term priority to a letter, for example.

To release a print job that has been paused, carry out the following steps in the printer control window.

1 In the *Document Name* column, click on the print job you want.

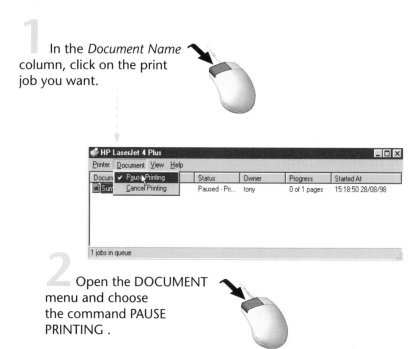

2 Open the DOCUMENT menu and choose the command PAUSE PRINTING .

You will see if a print job is paused by the check mark next to the command. Clicking the command again will release the job. Windows searches through the list of print jobs from top to bottom and outputs the next released print job to the printer.

Sometimes it is necessary to cancel a print job. Perhaps you selected the function by mistake or there was a printer error during printing and you had to turn off the device to rectify the error. Only a couple of steps are required to cancel a print job:

1 In the *Document Name* column click on the print job you want.

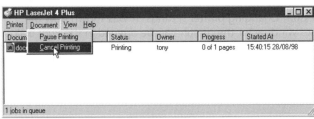

2 Open the DOCUMENT menu and choose the command CANCEL PRINTING.

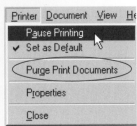

It takes a few seconds for the job to be cancelled and for the updated list to be displayed.

To cancel all print jobs it is easier to choose the command PURGE PRINT DOCUMENTS in the PRINTER menu.

In this menu you can also choose the command PAUSE PRINTING. Windows will then interrupt the printout. This is particularly useful if there is either no printer currently attached or the printer is temporaily unusable.

TIP

In the PRINTER menu you can also tell whether the device is set up as the default printer. In this case a small check mark (tick) appears in front of the command SET AS DEFAULT. If this check mark is missing, simply click the command and Windows will set the device as the default printer.

TIP

In the lesson "Changing printer settings" it was shown how the Properties window for the printer can be opened in the *Print* dialog box by clicking the *Properties* button. You can also click the command PROPERTIES in the PRINTER menu (of the printer control window for the particular printer); the Properties window now contains additional tabs for separator page/comments/test page (*General*) and connections settings (*Details*).

233

7
Having fun with Windows

What's in this chapter?

You can use Windows not only for work but also for entertainment or for relaxation. A keyword here is "games" which can really be fun in Windows. Or perhaps you would rather listen to music CDs whilst working on the computer? This is no problem either. Playing films and video sequences is just as easy in Windows. In this chapter you will find out how all this is done.

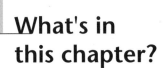

You already know about:

You are going to learn about:

Playing music CDs on the computer

Is your computer fitted with a CD-ROM drive? If so, you can play music CDs whilst working on the computer. All you need is a pair of headphones connected to the headphone jack on the CD drive. On some computers with an integral sound card, playing music CDs also works via the sound card loudspeaker. For playing music CDs, Windows provides a program whose operation is explained below.

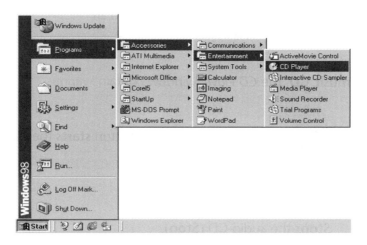

1 Open the Start menu and click PROGRAMS followed by ACCESSORIES.

2 In the group ENTERTAINMENT click on CD PLAYER.

Windows starts the CD Player
program, which responds as
shown in the window opposite.

 Now insert a music CD (also called an
audio CD) in the drive.

To **play** the **music CD**, the *CD Player* window contains various
buttons.

 With an audio CD inserted, this button **starts** the player
(**Play**).

 Temporarily **stops** play (**Pause**).

 Stops the audio-CD (**Stop**).

 Opens the **drawer** of the CD-ROM drive (**Eject**).

 To move backwards (**Skip Backward**) or forwards (**Skip
Forward**) within a music track.

To move to the **Previous Track** or the **Next Track**.

You might already know these buttons from your CD player. The real
power of the CD Player program supplied with Windows lies in the fact
that you can compile your own list of CD music tracks to play.

1 In the CD Player window click *Edit Play List.*

The program now opens a window in which you can **input** the options for the **tracks** of the **CD.**

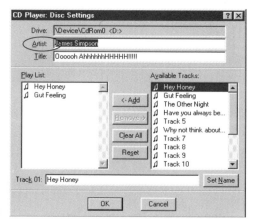

2 Click the *Artist* box and enter the artist's name.

3 Click the *Title* box and type in the title of the CD.

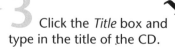

The texts you have entered are displayed in the CD Player window.

Maybe the toolbar is missing from your CD Player window or you can't see the Artist and Title? You will find (toggle-action) commands in the VIEW menu for showing/hiding these and other elements in the window (e.g. the toolbar).

On first being activated, the program lists all the **music tracks on the CD** as *Track 01, Track 02* and so on. In the next step you can enter the track titles into the list. To do this proceed as follows:

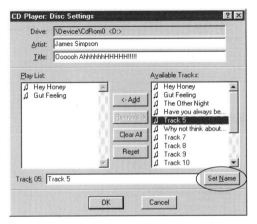

1 In the list *Available Tracks,* click the track you want to enter.

2 Then click the *Track* box.

3 Type in the name of the track.

4 Click the *Set Name* button.

239

The program accepts the name of the track you typed in and selects the next track in the list. If necessary, you can repeat the various steps and so enter all the tracks.

The **order** of play of the audio CD **tracks** can be specified in the *Play List* box on the left.

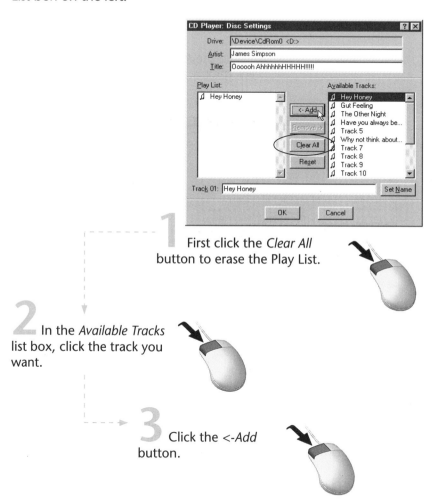

First click the *Clear All* button to erase the Play List.

In the *Available Tracks* list box, click the track you want.

Click the *<-Add* button.

The program adds the track to the Play List. Repeat each step until all the desired tracks are in the Play List.

To **remove** a **track** from the **Play List**, proceed as follows:

1 Open the *CD Player: Disc Settings* dialog box.

2 In the *Play List* box, click the track concerned.

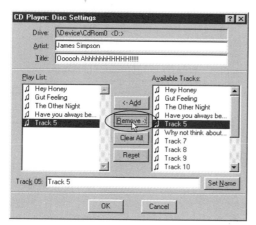

3 Then choose the *Remove->* button.

4 As soon as you have specified all the tracks to be removed, close the dialog box via the *OK* button.

If you now start the CD Player (see above), the program will play the chosen tracks in the order you have selected.

You also have the option of **choosing** a particular **track** directly from the CD Player dialog box.

1 Open the *Track* drop-down list box.

2 Click the track you want.

Here you can see the tracks we specified in the previous step.

Besides the buttons for playing the CD, the toolbar contains some more buttons to control the digital time display in the *CD Player dialog box*.

 The left button displays the **track time elapsed** for the current track. You use the right button to switch the display to the track time remaining.

 This button displays the **disc time remaining** for the whole **CD** in the digital display.

The group of the following three buttons affects the play of the audio CD. You can choose a button and then start the player. The program will then play in the mode chosen by the button.

Use this button to ouput the tracks from the **Play List in random order**.

 If you find it too tiresome to insert new CDs, choose the *continuous play* button. The **tracks** will then **play repeatedly** in the order shown in the Play List.

Do you just want to have a quick listen to the beginning of each track on a music CD in order to pick out an interesting track?

1 Click this button on the window toolbar.

2 Start the CD playing with this button.

The *CD Player* program will now play just the beginning of each track. This mode is also known as **Intro Play**.

To adjust the duration of Intro Play, proceed as follows:

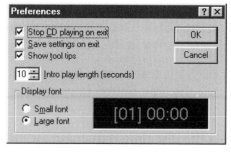

1 In the OPTIONS menu choose the command PREFERENCES.

2 In the *Preferences* dialog box, specify the *Intro play length*.

You can either type in this value (max. 15 seconds) or change it by clicking the buttons.

243

Working with sound files

Windows has a program called *Sound Recorder* that can be used to record and play back sound documents; these are saved in **sound files** which often have the extension *.wav*. The only requirement for playing sound documents is for your computer to be fitted with a sound card. To record sound documents, you will also need a microphone.

If a **sound card** is available for playing sound files, Windows will (normally) tell you by displaying a small speaker icon in the taskbar. Double-click on this icon to open the **Volume Control** window.

You start the Sound Recorder with a few mouse clicks:

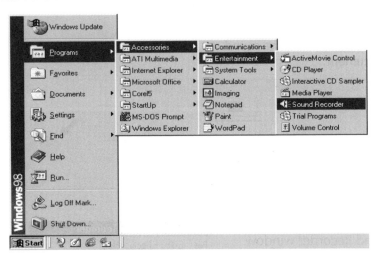

1 Open the Start menu and click PROGRAMS / ACCESSORIES.

2 Click ENTERTAINMENT followed by SOUND RECORDER.

Windows starts the program which responds as shown in the window opposite.

You can now **record** your own **sound documents**. To do this, proceed as follows:

1 Turn on the microphone and prepare to record.

2 To start recording, click this button.

3 Now record the sound document.

4 To stop recording, click this button.

The picture opposite shows the Sound Recorder window after recording has been stopped.

245

You can now play back, edit and save the recording. We have already mentioned that sound documents are stored in files with the extension *.wav*. To save, carry out the following steps:

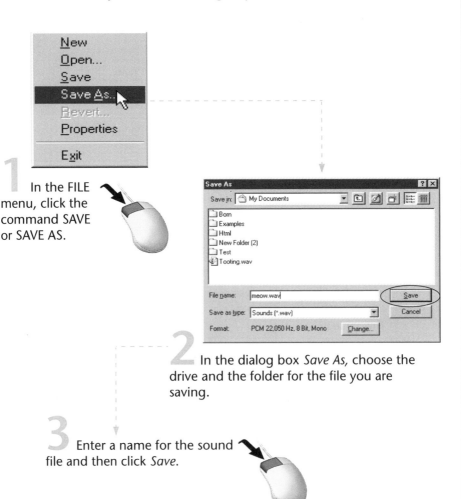

1 In the FILE menu, click the command SAVE or SAVE AS.

2 In the dialog box *Save As,* choose the drive and the folder for the file you are saving.

3 Enter a name for the sound file and then click *Save*.

The Sound Recorder will now store the current sound document in the file you have specified. If at a later stage you choose the command SAVE, the sound document will be saved without further enquiry. However, by means of the command SAVE AS you can save the sound document under a new filename.

Sound documents can be saved in different ways and at different **qualities** (telephone, radio, CD). The better the quality, the larger the sound file. In the *Save As* dialog box you will find the *Change* button. This opens the *Sound Selection* dialog box in which you can specify the quality in the *Name* box.

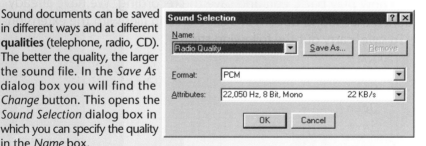

If you have **sound files**, they can be **played** in the Sound Recorder. You will need to load the file you want and then play.

In the Sound Recorder menu, click on FILE and then the command OPEN.

Specify the drive and the folder in which the .*wav*-files are stored.

247

3 Click on the file you want and then on the *Open* button.

4 Click the *Play* button.

The sound document will now play. The length of the sound document and the time already run are displayed in the Sound Recorder window.

1 To **stop playing**, click the Stop button .

In the Sound Recorder window there is a Position slider which can be moved during playback. You can also move this slider with the mouse to any position you wish in the sound document.

In this way you can also go to the beginning or end of the sound document: however, it is smarter to use the following two buttons:

Positions at the **beginning** of the sound document.

Positions at the **end** of the sound document.

Via the two menus EDIT and EFFECTS, the Sound Recorder provides functions for changing sound documents at a later stage. You can "cut" a sound document, alter its playback speed, reverse it or mix it with other sound documents. For details on these functions, refer to Help on the Sound Recorder.

Working with sound documents is fun, but its strength only becomes evident if you insert a recording of your own voice in a text document and pass it on. The recipient can then retrieve the recorded sound directly from the loaded text document. At the end of Chapter 4 you will find an example of what this might look like in WordPad.

Looking at videos in Windows

Windows has a program called *Media Player*. You can of course use this program to play audio CDs or, as with Sound Recorder, playback sound documents from *.wav*-files. In this lesson we shall, however, mainly be dealing with the considerably more interesting functions for playing video files. This will enable you to effectively convert your computer into a "home cinema". Using a computer of an appropriate speed (e.g. a 133MHz Pentium PC) with an integal sound card, the videos will fill the screen and be output with sound. There is now a huge number of CDs containing these video files.

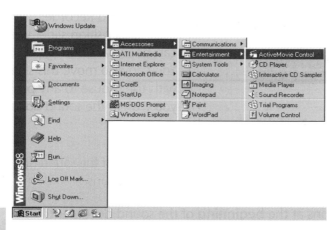

To start the program, click in the Start menu on PROGRAMS / ACCESSORIES.

2 In the ACCESSORIES submenu, choose the entry ENTERTAINMENT followed by MEDIA PLAYER.

The Media Player program responds with a relatively simple window.

The buttons in the toolbar work as for the CD Player program already described at the beginning of the chapter.

| | **Starts play** of an audio CD, a sound document or a video. |

| | **Pauses play**. This button appears instead of the *Play* button as soon as the player starts. |

| | **Stops play** of an audio CD, a sound document or a video. |

| | **Ejects a CD**. A second mouse click on this button recloses the CD drawer. |

| | These buttons are for **rewind** and **fast forward** respectively. You can then move the play mark incrementally in a CD track, in an audio file or in a video. |

| | These buttons are for moving to the previous mark and next mark respectively. They switch between different tracks of a music CD, take you to the beginning or end of a sound document or position a video at selection marks (the beginning or end of the video or of a defined section). |

The operation of the Media Player program is as easy as for the CD Player. On the Windows CD-ROM you will even find a few *.avi-* and *.mpg-*files in the *cdsample**videos* folder so you can try out playing video files.

1 Click on the DEVICE menu and choose the device you want.

2 If there is no check mark in front of the commands VIDEO FOR WINDOWS... or ACTIVE MOVIE... , click the item concerned.

3 In the FILE menu, choose the command OPEN.

4 Search for the *cdsample**videos* folder on the Windows CD-ROM.

5 If necessary, set the video file format using the FILES OF TYPE drop-down list box.

251

Open

Look in: videos

barneysw.avi   picture.avi
flaglobe.avi
gamepad.avi
golf3.avi
greeting.avi
msn.avi

File name: golf3.avi   Open

Files of type: Video for Windows (*.avi)   Cancel

6 Click one of the video files and then
the *Open* button.

golf3.avi - Media Player (stopped)

File Edit Device Scale Help

0.00 2.00 4.00 6.00 8.00 10.00 12.00 14.00   17.80

00.00 (sec)

Play golf3.avi

7 Click the *Play* button.

The video is now displayed in a second window. You can stop the play
at any time by using the buttons described above or by clicking Rewind
or Fast Forward.

Do you find it annoying that the video window is displayed on the screen only in postage stamp or postcard size? The window can of course be resized in the usual way. But you can also adjust the size of the window used on start-up.

1 In the DEVICE menu, click on the command PROPERTIES.

2 Select the *Window* radio button.

3 Open the drop-down list box and choose the window size you want.

4 Close the Video tab via the *OK* button.

You can select the video playback window size in various steps from the original size to maximised. Choose a size that optimises quality and playback speed.

If a specific section of a video interests you, you can specify this as a selection.

1 Start the video playing.

2  At the start of the selection click this button (Start Selection).

3 Select the end of the clip with this button (End Selection).

golf3.avi - Media Player (stopped)
File Edit Device Scale Help

0.00 2.00 4.00 6.00 8.00 10.00 12.00 14.00 17.80

08.30 (sec)

The required selection is marked as a blue bar in the position slider display which shows the current play position.

Via the command SELECTION in the EDIT menu, a selection can also be specified in frame mode. The command OPTIONS in the EDIT menu opens a dialog box in which you can, for example, choose *Auto Rewind* or *Auto Repeat*. Further information on the functions of the Media Player program can be found in its online Help. In addition to Media Player, you will also find the program ACTIVEMOVIE CONTROL in the same branch of the Start menu. This program works like Media Player and can also play videos.

Like pictures and sound documents, videos can also be inserted in a letter or text document. You can, for example, create a letter in WordPad and include a video. The user can then look at the file created by WordPad on the computer. However, bear in mind that video files are very large and that the letter might no longer fit on a diskette.

Minesweeper

Windows comes with the program *Minesweeper*. This is a game in which you have to find out the safe areas as quickly as possible.

The playing field is divided into various small boxes. By clicking on these you can find out if a box is clear of mines and whether there are mines in the vicinity.

A **number 1**in a box means that there is **one** mine in one of the **adjacent boxes**. The number 2 indicates that there are two mines in adjacent boxes.

To play Minesweeper, proceed as follows:

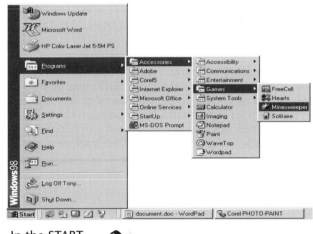

1 In the START menu, click on PROGRAMS and then ACCESSORIES.

2 Choose GAMES followed by the program MINESWEEPER.

Windows starts the game Minesweeper which responds as shown in the window opposite. Now you can begin "minesweeping".

1 Click on one of the boxes.

2 Click other "clear" boxes.

In each case, the **box** is **uncovered**. The objective is to uncover as many boxes as possible without hitting a mine, and to do this as quickly as possible.

If you choose a box with a mine in it then you lose the game (as in the picture here). The picture clearly shows how the numbers in the various boxes relate to the hidden mines. Incidentally, the time since sweeping started appears in the digital display at the top right.

TIP

Do you think there's a mine in a box? Then point with the mouse to another box that seems likely to be clear. If you now hold the left and right buttons down together, Minesweeper will uncover all adjacent boxes that are free of mines. On releasing the mouse buttons the boxes become covered again and you can then sweep these individually.

If you suspect there is a mine in a box, you can right-click it. Minesweeper will mark this box with a little flag.

Here you see some boxes that have been marked by **little flags**.

1 To start a new game, click on the face button.

Incidentally, this sort of face is often known as a **Smiley**.

WHAT'S THIS?

In computer technology, **Smileys** are often used to express emotions (such as smiling, sadness, anger etc.). The button in Minesweeper shows three different versions of the Smiley character. In electronic messages (e-mail), normal characters are used for representing Smileys (see Chapter 8).

TIP

In the Game menu you will find various commands for beginning a new game and setting the level of difficulty. Further information can be obtained by clicking the Help button.

Relaxing with Solitaire

Solitaire is a card game that has been reproduced in Windows in the form of a computer game. The objective is to build up from the deck four stacks of cards, in suits, in the order ace to King.

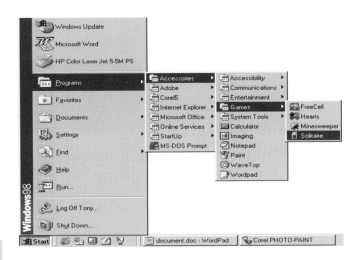

1 In the Start menu, choose PROGRAMS followed by ACCESSORIES.

2 In the menu ACCESSORIES choose the group GAMES.

3 Click on SOLITAIRE.

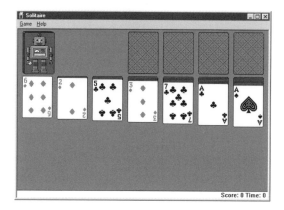

4 On first activating the program, the cards are automatically laid out. To begin a new game, click the GAME menu and then the command DEAL.

The program now deals a new set of cards from the deck.

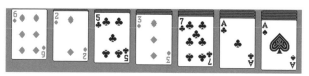

On the bottom row you see seven stacks with the top cards turned face up. You can use the mouse to drag face up cards onto a suitable stack.

The card deck with the rest of the cards is face down in the top left corner.

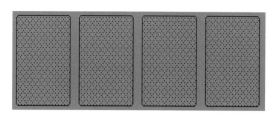

The positions of the four suit stacks are also marked in the top right corner; you build these up in ascending order, starting with the ace.

259

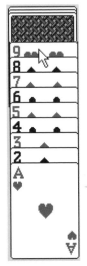

1 To draw cards, click the deck in the top left corner.

2 Face up cards can be removed from one stack and dragged with the mouse to another suitable stack on the bottom row.

3 If there is an ace face up on the top of a card stack, double-click it and put it down on one of the four suit stacks.

4 If the top card on a stack is face down, turn it over by double-clicking.

In the course of the game you have to make valid moves in this way and lay the cards on the stacks, sorted in order; the cards in a stack have to be alternately red and black.

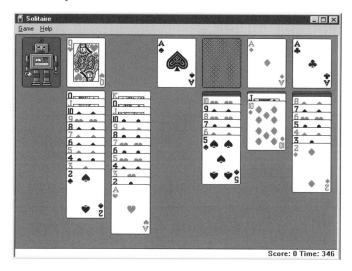

In addition, the order of the cards must be maintained (King, Queen, Jack, ten, nine, eight, seven, six, five, four, three, two, ace). This means that over a black five of Spades you can only have a red four of Hearts or red four of Diamonds. Invalid moves are rejected by the program. The game ends either after you have arranged all the cards into suit stacks or no further valid moves are possible.

Further information on playing the game is given in the Help text for the program, which you can call by clicking the Help button. From the GAME menu, various commands are available for dealing, undoing the last move and for setting options. Windows contains other card games such as FreeCell and Hearts. In the folder \cdsample you will also find information on the games that are available from Microsoft.

The command DECK in the GAME menu opens a window called *Select Card Back* in which you can choose the design for the deck. Use the "Robot" deck and see what happens.

What's in this chapter?

Are you connected to the Internet? Would you like to know what the Internet and the World Wide Web are? Are you interested in what lies behind the terms channel bar and e-mail? Then this is the chapter to read. Here you will find out how to surf the World Wide Web. The functions for this are already available in the form of Microsoft Internet Explorer in Windows. Furthermore, this chapter will tell you about the basic terms concerning the Internet and will show how you can send e-mail (really electronic post). This knowledge can also be applied when working on the Intranets now used in many firms. So you don't have access to the Internet? Still no problem: you will be using this knowledge to look at HTML documents which are becoming ever more common on CD-ROMs.

You already know about:

You are going to learn about:

Internet, Intranet, World Wide Web and browsers

The **Internet** is something that everybody is now talking about, but do you actually know what is behind this collective term? The word combines the two terms *Inter(national)* and *Net(work)*. It therefore has something to do with a global network.

In the Internet, this idea has been persistently pursued: not only have computers within a company been interconnected, but so have computers in different towns and countries.

For example, a computer in San Francisco can exchange data with another in Rome or Rio. These systems are mostly interconnected via the public telephone network or via data circuits (in some cases by satellite).

San Francisco

Rome

Rio

Originally, only a few computers in various universities were connected by the Internet. Anyone with access to such a computer could reach all other computers on the Internet (and hence the users of these computers). To send a file or message to another user, you only need an address, just like with the post. Because exchanging data on the Internet is very easy, fast and inexpensive, more and more computers have been connected world-wide. Today, the Internet consists of many thousands of computers in institutions, government departments and companies. These computers are often also called Web servers.

But what can you do on the Internet and what advantages are there in all this? Like the early post office (which you could use to make telephone calls, send letters and parcels and carry out financial transactions) the Internet provides various services (such as exchanging messages, sending files, making telephone calls and so on). It is therefore no problem to visit a computer at NASA in the USA, to enquire about the weather forecast for Mallorca or to send an electronic mail to a friend in Australia, all from your living room. In a **chat room** you can converse with participants throughout the world. With the right equipment configuration, you can even hold online conferences with simultaneous interpretation over the Internet. The Windows Program NetMeeting supports this form of conversation. **Newsgroups** allow the exchange of information on every topic imaginable.

There is a huge number of special Internet functions that cannot be dealt with here. The majority of Internet users only actually make use of two functions: sending **e-mail** and "surfing" the **World Wide Web**. Windows 98 also supports Internet services such as **Chat** and **Newsgroups** (which will not be dealt with in this book).

There still remain a couple of questions: **How does the World Wide**

WHAT'S THIS?

E-mail is nothing other than electronic letters. You write a text on the computer, enter the recipient and send this message as an **e-mail** to the nearest Internet computer. For this you only need a telephone connection and a **modem** which is a device for transmitting messages over a telephone line. The Internet ensures that the message is made available to the recipient in a **mailbox**. The recipient can load, read, edit and forward the message on his computer. You can attach other files to an e-mail that are forwarded with the message. E-mail is cost-effective as you only pay the subscription charge for the Internet and the cost of a local telephone call to the nearest Internet computer. Long-distance telphone call charges are therefore not incurred as is the case when sending faxes. E-mail is fast (compared with the postal service): a message is usually with the recipient after just a few minutes.

The **World Wide Web** (or just "Web") is another service via which **Web pages** can be retrieved. These pages may contain the latest weather report, stockmarket rates or advertising for a particular company. To view Web pages you need a special program known as a **browser**. Microsoft Internet Explorer is the default browser used in Windows.

The Internet offers **chat rooms**, in which like-minded individuals can "meet" and chat about anything under the sun. However, chatting is restricted to the exchange of short texts. The Chat service is therefore a form of entertainment which takes place online, with all participants having to visit the chat room on the Internet at the same time. A modern variant is offered by the Windows program **NetMeeting**, which allows participation in Internet conferences if you have a sound card and microphone.

Newsgroups are discussion groups on particular topics on the Internet. Participants can select information on various topics as text pages as well as ask questions or give answers to questions that others have asked. This facilitates the exchange of information worldwide. Unlike chats, which take place online, contributions remain in Newsgroups for some time (weeks or months) and can still be read by other participants some while later.

Besides the term "**Internet**", the word "**Intranet**" crops up ever more frequently. Intranets are networks that use the same programs as the Internet and are often used in big companies. As these networks can only be used by company staff, the name **Inter** has been swapped for the term **Intra**. If you are familiar with the Internet functions, you can proceed immediately on a company Intranet.

Web work? And what is so **special about the Web** that makes it so popular? We will now present a few thoughts on this. In the Internet there are many thousands of computers on which countless files are stored. This obviously causes some problems when searching for particular documents. Just think of searching for a particular file on your own computer. How would this work with many millions of users? Having finally found the external document, you might not be able to read it because it was created with an unknown program (would you know what word processor someone is currently using in far-off India and would you by chance have it installed on your computer?).

To simplify finding and displaying documents, the **World Wide Web** (**WWW** or just **Web** for short) was created. Although document files are also dispersed on computers throughout the world, each **document** has an **address** which clearly defines where the associated file can be found (you can think of this address as being like the address on a letter). In addition, all **documents** are stored in a **special format** with the file extension *.htm* or *.html*. There are programs such as Microsoft Internet Explorer which can read and display these files. These programs are generally known as **browsers**. These two features — address and file format — facilitate easy access to documents using a browser.

WHAT'S THIS?

In this connection you will probably come across the term **HTML**. This stands for **Hypertext Markup Language**; it is used to create documents so that they can be displayed on different computers by a browser. HTML documents are (mostly) stored in files with the extensions *.htm* or *.html*.

The HTML language allows you to place references to other documents in a document. These references are called **hyperlinks**. On finding such a reference in an HTML document, a mouse click is all that is needed to load the related document.

TIP

If you do not create documents for the Web yourself, you will not need to concern yourself with the **HTML** language and its subtleties. However, this language enables providers of Web pages to create a chain of different documents. For this purpose, Windows includes the program FrontPage Express, which you can use to modify HTML documents or create your own Web pages.

267

If you know the address of an HTML document, it can be specified in the browser, which will then load the document from the World Wide Web (or from the Intranet or from a drive on the local computer) and display it on your computer.

As a reader, it may not matter to you where the files are stored. Once you have tracked down an interesting Web page in the Internet, you can get to other pages via hyperlinks. The browser searches the document of the chosen hyperlink independently in the Web and downloads it to your computer from one in Rome, Tokyo or Sydney as needed. Switching like this between different Web pages is also known as **surfing the Internet**. How this actually works will become apparent in the following lessons.

First steps with Internet Explorer

Did you read the previous section and find it all double Dutch? Do you find the whole thing terribly complicated? If so, then you should read the following words of encouragement:

➡ The first good news is: don't worry — surfing Web pages is child's play and opens up entirely new worlds. And the browser which you need to "surf the net" is already included in Windows 98 as **Microsoft Internet Explorer**. So you can get started right away and call up your first Web pages.

➡ Because this is all so simple, Microsoft has integrated many Internet functions directly into Windows; this means you will already know some of the functions (although perhaps you don't yet realise this – for instance, if you are using Windows Help, there is a sort of HTML document behind it).

➡ The bad news is: to surf the Web, you do need access to the Internet. Such access is provided by online service providers such as CompuServe, America Online (AOL), T-Online, Microsoft Network (MSN), Metronet and others.

➡ Perhaps you don't have an Internet connection or you are not online? In which case "surfing the Net" will certainly be out for today; but do not give up. The good news is that if there are HTML documents stored on your computer, you can retrieve these in the same way in Internet Explorer. In the future, CD-ROMs will increasingly supply documents in the HTML format.

To enable all readers, with or without an Internet connection, to make a start, I have prepared a "dry-run surf course" for the first steps. For this you only need your Windows 98 CD-ROM. This contains some HTML documents used for the basic steps. So, even if you are not yet online, you should nevertheless make an attempt and try out the following steps.

To display a Web document, you have two options:

➡ Start Microsoft Internet Explorer and specify where the document is that you want to find.

➡ If the Web document is saved as an HTML file on a drive of your computer, open the relevant folder (for example, via the desktop icon *My Computer*). All you need to do then is double-click on the HTML file in order to start Internet Explorer and to load the document.

For the following steps the first option has been chosen since it allows both access to pages in the World Wide Web as well as the display of local files. That's enough of the preliminaries; let's go to our first Web page.

1   Insert the Windows 98 CD-ROM into the drive.

Now Microsoft Internet Explorer needs to be launched. Although you will find the entry for this program in the Start menu in the menu PROGRAMS / INTERNET EXPLORER, it's much too laborious to call up the program via the Start menu.

269

Internet Explorer

Launch Internet Explorer Browser

2 Launch (start) the
program by clicking the
mouse on the icon in the
Quick Launch toolbar.

If there is an icon for the program on the desktop, you can also launch
Internet Explorer by double-clicking this.

The program opens the window
opposite to display the home
page. In this example the
home page is blank.

Does this window seem familiar
to you? The title and menu bars
resemble the display in a folder
window.

In the title bar, the message
"[Working Offline]" shows that there is still no connection to the Internet.
The only difference is that the toolbar contains a few different buttons.
The Address toolbar is also found in a folder window.

After launch, does Internet Explorer immediately
try to establish connection with the Internet and
show an error to the effect that the address cannot
be found? In this case the wrong **home page** is
set. We will explain how to change this page
below.

Now you just have to
tell the **browser** where
to find the Web page.
To start off, we shall use
one of the pages stored
on the Windows 98
CD-ROM.

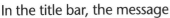

3 In the FILE menu choose the command OPEN or press the key combination Ctrl + O.

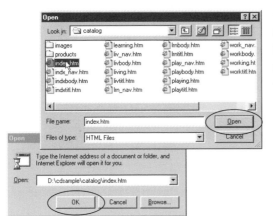

Internet Explorer now shows (lower left in the illustration opposite) the dialog box *Open*, whose text box, also labelled *Open*, is still blank.

4 Click the *Browse* button.

5 In the top dialog box *Open*, that has just opened, choose the folder *\cdsample\catalog* which is on the Windows CD-ROM.

6 Select the file *index.htm*, and click the *Open* button.

The *Open* text box (in the lower dialog box) now contains the path to the chosen HTML document.

7 Click the *OK* button in the bottom dialog box *Open*.

271

Internet Explorer loads the specified HTML document and displays its contents.

Here you see the home page from the Microsoft Catalog showing the different products in the form of an index. These products appear as **underlined text**. This is how **hyperlinks** are **represented**.

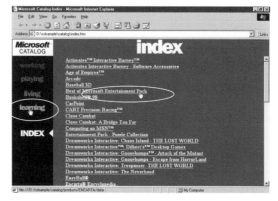

1 Point to one of these hyperlinks.

The mouse pointer assumes the form of a stylised hand and you will find the address of the next page entered in the browser status bar.

Hyperlinks don't always have to be underlined text, however: graphics can also contain hyperlinks. You see this, for example, if you point to the entries for categories such as "learning", "index" etc. on the left hand side of the page. You can get to related pages via these hyperlinks.

2 Click the hyperlink "Encarta® Encyclopedia".

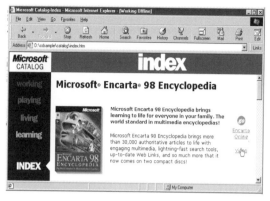

The browser calls up the document referred to in the hyperlink. Here you see the page with the product description for Microsoft Encarta 98.

This page contains further hyperlinks. For instance, click on the "Video" hyperlink and the browser will open the video player window and present a video of the product. The "Encarta Online" hyperlink refers directly to the Microsoft Web page. Without an Internet connection, however, you will not be able to visit this page.

Now use the scroll bar slider to scroll to the end of the Web page.

At the end of the page you will see some references to related products. Clicking on these will bring you to the relevant page. But suppose we now want to get back to the start of the page. Should we scroll back? No — there is a more elegant way.

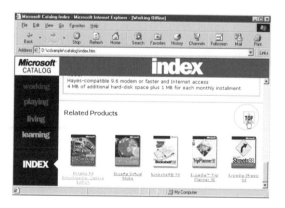

Click the icon "Top".

273

Internet Explorer now displays the top of the page again. You have just met the second form of a hyperlink. The author of the document can insert such hyperlinks to make it easier for the reader to scroll through the document (also known as navigating) and to guide him or her directly to specific places in the current page. A great many Web pages contain hyperlinks that refer back to the top of a page.

5 Now click in the left region of the window on the entry "learning".

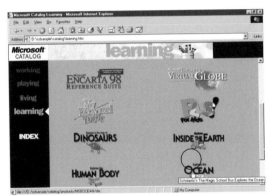

The browser shows the overview page opposite with a number of graphics which are also hyperlinks. Point to one of these graphics and Internet Explorer displays a text label with information about the next page.

6 Click in the bottom right of the window on "The Magic School Bus Explores the Ocean".

Internet Explorer displays the relevant Web page where you will find further hyperlinks.

7 Now experiment with changing the size of the window.

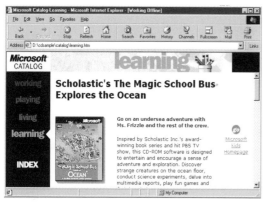

The browser automatically adjusts the text width to the window width. For **Web pages** there is **no fixed page size.**

8 Scroll down until the view opposite appears.

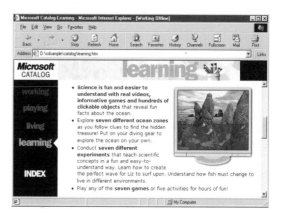

Look at the "screen" shown on the Web page: after a few seconds the theme displayed will change. This is another refinement in Web documents.

Besides the videos already mentioned, an author of Web pages can place animated graphics in a page that convey the impression of movement.

Did you go through the above steps? It didn't hurt at all, did it?

There are however another couple of questions that you will come across sooner or later. Let's suppose you want to go back again to the **page last visited**. Does this mean you now have to type in the original Web address for this page in the *Address* box or call it up via the dialog box *Open*? No, you won't, as the browser keeps track. It automatically records the addresses of the Web pages you have visited.

1 Click *Back* in the toolbar.

The browser now displays the previous Web page again. In this example the browser will open the page just visited showing the products currently on offer.

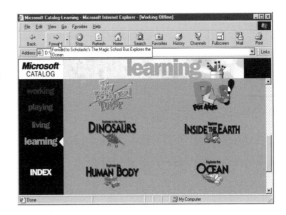

And if you want to move forward?

2 Click on the *Forward* button.

On pointing to a button, information on the page referred to appears in a text label.

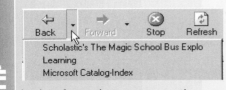

The two buttons *Forward* and *Back* only work if you have already visited more than one page in the current session. The next time you launch, the buttons will be "greyed out". The browser can only page back or forward one page at a time, so you might have to do a lot of clicking to get back to a particular page. However, you can open the menu for these buttons (by right-clicking them) and directly retrieve one of the pages you visited before.

You will see that surfing Web pages really is child's play. The most difficult thing is knowing the correct address for the home page (but more on that later). Perhaps you would like to do a little more surfing in the Web pages of the Windows 98 CD-ROM?

Some of the products described are contained as trial versions on the Windows 98 CD-ROM. To install, go to the Start menu and choose the entry PROGRAMS / ACCESSORIES / ENTERTAINMENT / TRIAL PROGRAMS. The program lets you interactively install multiple trial versions of the software products.

The Web pages of the catalogue on the Windows CD-ROM have been divided into several windows (also called panes). So in the left pane you see the column with entries such as "index", "learning" etc., which makes navigation easier for you. How a document is laid out, whether a window is divided into panes and where hyperlinks are placed depends, however, on the particular content provider.

Getting online

Were you able to understand the example in the previous lesson? Do you have an appetite for more? Then it's time to visit your first Web pages on the Internet. This is no more difficult than surfing on the Windows 98 CD-ROM.

For the following lessons you will need a working connection to the Internet. If you install AOL, T-Online or CompuServe, these connections will be automatically set up. In the case of AOL, you will first have to start the access software and log in. Once online, the Internet can be accessed from Windows 98. You can also use this trick with CompuServe or T-Online, if Microsoft Internet Explorer reports an error in accessing the Internet.

Before carrying out the following steps, make sure that your modem is connected to the computer and to the telephone socket, and that it is switched on. If you have ISDN access, you must be able to use it for the online link.

1 Launch Internet Explorer
(e.g. by a mouse click on the button in
the Quick Launch toolbar).

Now you have to tell the browser where to find the document you want. This is done by directly typing into the *Address* box. Addresses are mostly entered in the following form:

http://www.xxx.com

The characters *http://* show that the document is on the Web (or on an Intranet). They are followed by a sequence of letters with the actual address.

The only difficulty is this is that you must know the exact address. The addresses of Web pages can, for example, be found in company advertisements. There are also magazines and other sources that publish such addresses. The following table contains some Web addresses (though these may change with time).

Sometimes the term **URL** also crops up in this connection. This stands for "Uniform Resource Locator" which is the Internet address.

www.stones.com	for Rolling Stones fans
www.tecno.com	for techno music enthusiasts
www.cnn.com	CNN news channel
www.bbc.co.uk	BBC
www.itv.co.uk	ITV
www.bbc.co.uk.radio1	BBC Radio 1
www.kissfm.com	Kiss FM radio
www.bt.com	British Telecom

www.cableandwireless.com	Cable and Wireless
www.nationalgeographic.com	National Geographic magazine
www.parliament.uk	for followers of the UK political scene
www.zone.com	for online games

Enter the address of a document, if you know it, in the browser *Address* box. The document will then be loaded. If necessary, you can then reach the following pages by means of the hyperlinks already mentioned.

1 In the Internet Explorer window, click the *Address* box.

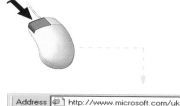

Enter the above URL address.

3 Press the ⏎ key to start access to the Web page.

The browser checks whether you have already visited this page. If the page is not found in the temporary storage, the message opposite will appear.

279

4 Click the *Connect* button.

It may be a few seconds before the browser finds the page required. Always bear in mind that the document might have to be fetched from the other end of the world. As a user, though, you don't need to worry about this. Just type the correct address into the browser.

If the address has been entered correctly, the browser will (normally) find the document and load it into your computer. The relevant page will then be built up step by step in the browser window. Depending on the size of the document and the number of graphics in it, this can take quite a long time.

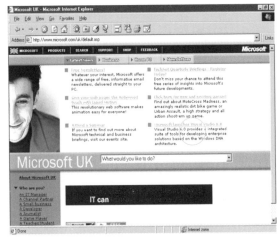

The picture opposite shows the Web page *http://www. microsoft.com/uk/default.asp*, in which Microsoft has assembled topical information on various subjects.

Choosing a hyperlink makes the related page appear. Here you see the next page with yet more hyperlinks, which in turn lead to other documents. The content provider of these pages can therefore use such hyperlinks to assemble a collection of documents for readers.

TIP

When you no longer want to "surf" on the Internet, you should disconnect your computer. Otherwise **telephone** and **online access charges** will continue to mount. Often (though not always!) it is sufficient to close the window of Internet Explorer to end the connection. If necessary, you can obtain further information from online access providers.

Loading Web pages via channels

Do you still find accessing Web pages too complicated? Microsoft Windows 98 goes some way to help you here. By using the **channel bar** you can get direct access to predefined Web content. Windows

remembers the **Web addresses** of pages listed in the **channel bar** for various content providers. But where is this channel bar?

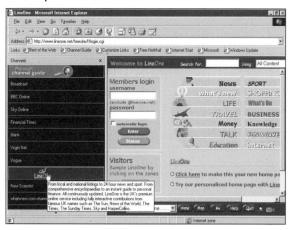

The picture opposite shows you where to find the **channel bar**: on **the desktop** and **in the Internet Explorer window.**

To retrieve one of these channel pages from the Web using Internet Explorer, a mouse click on a channel entry is all that is required. The LineOne page has been chosen here.

Is the channel bar missing from your desktop or Internet Explorer window?

 In Internet Explorer, the channel bar can be toggled in or out in the left pane of the window via the *Channels* button.

If the channel bar is hidden on your desktop, carry out the following steps:

1 Right-click with the mouse on a free area of the desktop and, in the context menu, choose the command PROPERTIES.

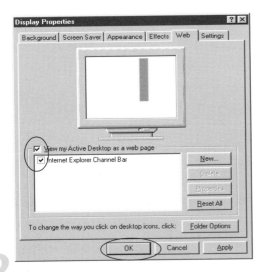

2 On the *Web* tab, select the check boxes *Internet Explorer Channel Bar* and *View my Active Desktop as a Web page*.

3 Close the tab via the *OK* button.

Click the *View Channels* button on the *Quick Launch* toolbar to open the Internet Explorer window in full-screen view with channel bar.

A Web page chosen via the channel bar can be treated like any other page. By using hyperlinks you can get to other pages related to the product of interest.

Marking Web pages

Perhaps there is a Web page that you visit frequently or which is a particular favourite? Then it's pretty tiresome to type in its address every time. Unfortunately, it's easy to forget the addresses of so many interesting Web pages (writing them down is too much effort). Microsoft Internet Explorer possesses a function which you can use to keep the addresses of interesting Web pages. This is sometimes also called **bookmarking** because a symbolic bookmark is effectively inserted between the pages in the Web so that you can look them up again later. In Internet Explorer this function is called *Favorites*. There are different ways of adding Web pages to your list of favourites. The easiest of these is as follows:

Click the *Favorites* button.

Internet Explorer now displays the Explorer bar with your favourite pages already specified in the left part of the window.

2 Call up the Web page you want in Internet Explorer.

3 Drag the document icon  from the *Address* box of the *Address* toolbar to where you want it in the Explorer bar.

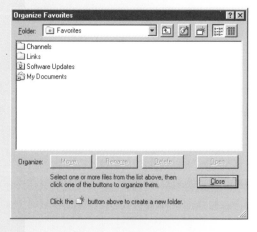

TIP

Alternatively, to specify a new entry you can choose the command ADD TO FAVORITES in the FAVORITES menu.

The new name is now inserted in the list of favourites. You can retrieve the Web page at a later time by choosing the relevant entry.

TIP

If you want to define a number of favourites, it is better to arrange these in groups (folders). To do this, choose the command ORGANIZE FAVORITES in the FAVORITES menu. The *Organize Favorites* dialog box lets you delete and rename favourites and to create folders for filing them.

WHAT'S THIS?

All the time your computer is connected to the Internet, it is said to be **online**. You should be aware of this since telephone and online charges are being incurred. When the connection is ended, the computer is **offline**.

Have you forgotten to create the appropriate favourite entries? Perhaps you've just visited a page but would prefer to read it later at your leisure? Here again Internet Explorer can normally help you, as you can also read pages **offline**.

The browser remembers the content of the pages you have visited and puts it into internal temporary storage which is maintained for a number of days. If you have been choosing different pages during an online session on the Internet by means of the *Back* and *Forward* buttons, the browser can load the page contents from its temporary storage. This speeds up displaying the Web pages. If you want to go offline and look at the content of pages you visited earlier, proceed as follows:

1 Click the *History* button.

In the Explorer bar, Internet Explorer shows the names of the Web pages visited, organised by days and weeks.

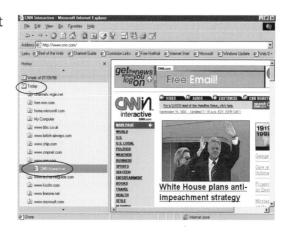

2 Click on a day of the week to display the entries.

3 Click one of these entries.

Internet Explorer now loads the page from internal storage. You can then read the page at your leisure.

Saving and printing pages

You might want to save a text page to look at it later. This can be done using Microsoft Internet Explorer in just a few steps:

1 In the FILE menu, click the command SAVE AS.

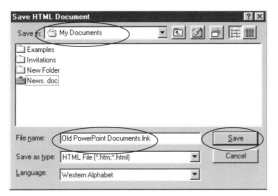

2 In the *Save As* dialog box, choose the folder in which you want to put the file.

3 Enter the filename in the box labelled *Filename*.

4 Click the *Save* button.

Internet Explorer will now save the text page as a file with the name you specified and the extension *.htm* or *.html*.

Unfortunately, using this method, pictures contained in the document cannot be saved along with the text. So what if you want to save a picture too?

1 Using the mouse, right-click on the picture.

287

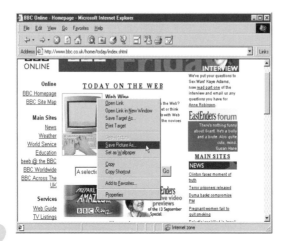

2 In the context menu, choose the command SAVE PICTURE AS and enter in the *Save picture* dialog box the filename and the folder for the picture.

The picture will be automatically filed together with its filename. Of course the browser will only be able to display the picture in the HTML document if the correct name for the picture folder has been used.

Perhaps you are wondering if you can reload a page saved in HTML format? This is no problem either. Since the HTML document format is increasingly popular, you will find more and more of these files on CD-ROMs or on program diskettes. How to load this kind of file has already been dealt with at the beginning of the chapter.

Printing loaded **HTML documents** is also fairly simple.

1 To print a page in Internet Explorer, click the *Print* button.

Internet Explorer will now print the page content.

2 If you require more control over the printout, choose the command PRINT in the FILE menu or press the key combination $\boxed{Ctrl} + \boxed{P}$.

3 Specify the options you want in the *Print* dialog box.

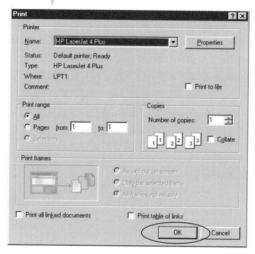

4 Click the OK button.

The browser will now print the content of the document page currently displayed together with graphics. The printout also includes those parts of the document that will not be seen if the display window is smaller than the document.

In the *Print* dialog box, select the check box "Print table of links". The browser will then print at the end of the document page a list of the addresses of all the hyperlinks in the document. This is a way of finding out interesting Web addresses.

Setting up the home page and other options

On starting Internet Explorer, its own start page is automatically loaded. This is the start page of a Web provider which is also commonly known as the **home page**.

 You also reach this home page as soon as you click this button in the toolbar.

This gives you the option of defining a page that you regularly use. If you lose your way when surfing in the Web jungle this button gets you back into familiar territory. Of course, you have to tell Internet Explorer in advance what home page you want to set. On Installation, the address of a Microsoft Web site is set as the default. To change the start address (and other options), proceed as follows:

1 Load the Web page in Explorer.

2 In the VIEW menu, click on the command INTERNET OPTIONS.

Internet Explorer now displays the properties window *Internet Options*.

3 Activate the *General* tab.

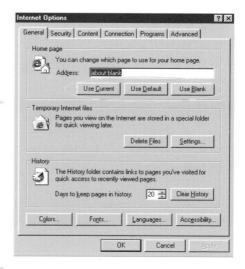

4 Choose one of the buttons in the *Home page* group.

5 Close the window via the *OK* button.

The *Use Blank* button sets the blank page that we showed at the beginning of this chapter as the home page. *Use Current* makes the currently loaded Web document the home page. Choosing *Use Default* sets the Microsoft home page address as your default home page.

As the home address, you can enter any valid Internet address as well as a file on your computer. Web addresses mostly begin with the letters *http://*, whereas a file on the hard disk of your computer is specified by the address *file://<Drive:Folder\File>* .

In the *History* group, you specify how many days Internet Explorer will temporarily store pages in the *History* folder. In addition, you can clear the contents of this folder via the *Clear History* button.

Searching the Web

The problem with accessing particular Web pages lies in the fact that you need to know their addresses. Given the millions of documents on the Web, this is some problem (at least in terms of volume). Fortunately there are so-called "**search engines**" which you can use to search for specific document content.

You can enter the URL address of such a search machine directly in the *Address* box of the *Address* toolbar. But who can really remember this sort of thing? Internet Explorer therefore assists you in your search by means of a predefined page.

1 Click the *Search* button in the Explorer toolbar.

Internet Explorer establishes a connection to the Internet and loads a search page in the left pane of the window.

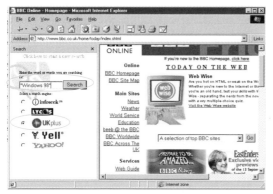

2 Type a keyword in the search text box.

3 Select the radio button for the search engine you want to use.

4 Click the *Search* button.

The search engine displays the documents it has found in the left pane of the window in short form together with hyperlinks.

5 Click one of the hyperlinks to display the related document in the right pane.

293

E-mail - what is it?

"Just give me your e-mail address". This sort of request is becoming ever more common and sending e-mail is routine for many people today. But what lies behind this term and how do you make use of this Internet function?

An **e-mail** is nothing other than the text of a letter that you send to a recipient in the form of an electronic message. As with a normal letter, you have to enter the address of the recipient and also your own as the sender. The Internet expects these in a special form of the type *name@courierservice.com*. For example, *hugox@aol.com* would be the way to address a message to a fictitious subscriber to America Online. The message you compose is subsequently forwarded on the Internet and stored in the recipient's **mailbox**. The recipient can then download it from the mailbox onto his or her computer before reading it.

Is Windows already set up on your computer for sending e-mails? If so, you can try out the following steps in Internet Explorer for creating and sending e-mail messages.

 Click the *Mail* button shown above on the Internet Explorer toolbar.

To receive an e-mail message, choose the command READ MAIL.

To write an e-mail message, choose the command NEW MESSAGE.

Internet Explorer now activates the program for editing e-mail messages; in Windows 98 this program is *Outlook Express.*

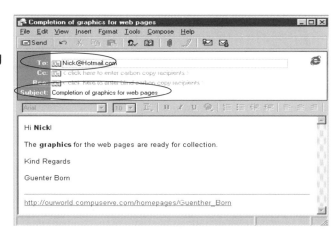

295

3 Click the *To* text box and enter the recipient's address.

If necessary, you can a enter a copy addressee in the *Cc* text box. Your sender's address will be automatically allocated by Outlook Express.

4 Click the *Subject* text box and enter a short reference to the message.

5 Click in the lower text area and type in the text of the message.

If required, you can also format the text using either the buttons shown above the top of the text window or the commands in the FORMAT menu. The command APPLY STATIONERY in the FORMAT menu lets you use a style of stationery for the background to the e-mail message.

E-mail messages often have characters like :-) which are generally known as **emoticons,** or **Smilies**. They are "faces" that have been rotated through 90 degrees to the left. They can be used to express emotion within the message (an e-mail is seldom as formal as a written letter). Smilies let you give the recipient an indication of the intention of the text. Here is a sample of a few Smilies:

:-) joy/humour   :-(sadness
;-) wink   :-o surprise/shock

6 ⌷☰ Send

Once you have created the message, click the *Send* button.

Your message will now be dispatched.

Depending on how your e-mail program *Outlook Express* is set up, the message will be sent directly to the Internet or temporarily stored in an out-basket; this allows messages to be collected and transmitted to the Internet node together. Note that Outlook Express cannot work with all online services. AOL users have to use the e-mail function provided by AOL access software. However, it is beyond the scope of this book to go into functions of Outlook Express.

Networking with Windows

What's in this chapter?

In companies, Windows is often used in networks to exchange data or files between individual computers or to share printers and hard disk drives. After reading this chapter you will be able to use Windows' networking functions. You will know how to log in to a network. In addition, you will learn how to print on the network and how to access the drives and folders of other computers on the network. You will also know how to enable drives, printers and folders on your PC to be shared by other network users.

You already know about:

You are going to learn about:

Networks — a brief overview

Perhaps you have already come across the term **network** (it has already cropped up in this book). Why do we need networks and what do they involve?

Let's suppose Frank Miller Design is a small architectural design firm employing several staff. There is Mr Miller, his secretary Jean Farmer and a second (part-time) partner, Peter Tyson. All have their own PCs, located in two separate rooms. Unfortunately there are a few snags. For cost reasons there are only two printers. When Peter wants to print something, he has to copy the files onto diskette and print from one of the other two PCs. Similar problems occur when Frank and Peter want to exchange drawings since the files are too big to fit on a diskette. You can well imagine that in larger firms these methods are simply not viable. Frank Miller has therefore decided to interconnect the individual PCs in the offices by cable in a **network**.

One possibility is to use one computer in effect as a **controlling station** (called a server) on the **network**. All files that need to be shared will be stored on this machine and the printer will also be attached to it. Every user on the network will be able to access the printer and the drives on the **server**.

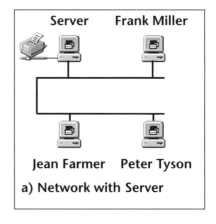

a) Network with Server

Servers are often used when a **large number of users** are working on a **network**. The server provides computing power for the network users. In addition, the network is administered by the server, which is a considerable advantage when there are more than 10 — 20 users. **Windows NT Server** and **Novell NetWare** are two products that are often used for PC network operations with servers.

However, it would be too complex and costly for Frank Miller to operate a dedicated server with all the associated software for the business. In fact, files are exchanged only occasionally and he would like to use all the computers. And he has just hired Jennie Andrews and bought another computer.

He therefore decides to go for a **workgroup network**. This also involves interconnecting the computers by cable. However, devices like printers can be attached to any PC. A user can now let other network users share his **resources**, such as the printer. In addition, drives and folders can be enabled for shared use.

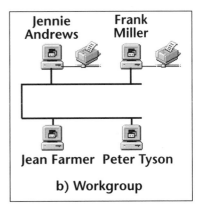

b) Workgroup

A **resource** in this context is a collective term for devices or entities that are available on a computer. Examples of devices are printers, floppy-disk drives, hard disk drives and CD-ROM drives. Examples of entities are folders and their subfolders. By way of simplification, the term 'resource' is therefore used in the network domain.

TIP

Since this type of network does not need its own server, it is often employed in smaller workgroups (small firms, departments and so on). Practically all that is needed is a cable and a **network card** for each PC for connection to the network. Workgroup network functions are already contained in Windows. This makes it possible to set up a very cost-effective network. Each user on the network decides what resources to enable on his computer for network sharing. Problems arise, though, if many users access the same computer and start using it at the same time. In addition, it is hardly efficient to manage a situation where individual users are making resources available for sharing when there are between 10 and 20 users.

To prevent unauthorised access to the server or workstations, each user must log in with a password (this has already been mentioned in Chapter 1). User names and passwords can be used, for example, to establish who is allowed to use which drives or printers.

How to network

If your computer is part of a network, it will support some additional functions for accessing network resources. You will notice the first difference on starting Windows. For computers already running on a **network**, for example, Windows expects you to log in when presented with the *Welcome to Windows* dialog box. This prevents unauthorised users accessing the network. Although you can bypass logging in by pressing the [Esc] key, not all Windows functions may then be available to you. To log in, proceed as follows:

Click the *User name* box
and type in your name.

2 In the second step, click in the *Password* box and enter your password.

3 Click the *OK* button.

The password characters are not displayed: instead only asterisks (*) are shown. This prevents outside persons being able to look over your shoulder and read the (secret) password. Once you have entered your name correctly and closed the dialog box via the *OK* button, you are in Windows and logged in to the network. (Don't be put off if your dialog box for logging-in looks slightly different from that shown here: this can be adjusted in Windows.)

TIP

The first time you log in, your name and password are stored. At the same time, a second dialog box appears in which you have to enter your new password again for confirmation. Take a note of your user name and password as you will need both the next time you log in. In networks there is often a specific person, usually called the **system administrator**, who is responsible for the operation of the computers. In this case, you must get your user name and password from the administrator.

The following paragraphs will describe in detail how to work with resources in a workgroup network. Working with a server is very much the same. If you get stuck when logging in or operating any of the network functions, ask your **system administrator** (this is the person responsible for the operation and administration of the network). You will also usually find out your user name and (confidential) password from this person.

After logging in to a Windows PC operating on a network, the *Network Neighborhood* icon will also appear on the desktop.

Network Neighborhood

You can use this icon to access the resources of other computers and, if required, printers, drives or folders. Operation is similar to working with the *My Computer* window.

Network Neighborhood

 Double-click the *Network Neighborhood* icon.

Windows now opens the *Network Neighborhood* window. This is similar in structure to the *My Computer* window with which you are already familiar. You can see a menu bar, a toolbar and a status bar. Working in this window is also similar to working in the *My Computer* window (see Chapter 3).

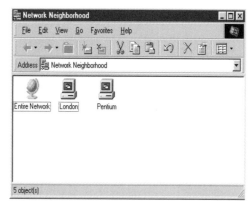

Only the icons within the *Network Neighborhood* window look somewhat different from those in the *My Computer* window. Whereas you can identify the drives on your computer in *the My Computer* window, the *Network Neighborhood* window contains network resources (that is to say, computers or stations).

Entire Network

Pentium

The *Entire Network* icon indicates the **workgroups** or servers within the whole network.

A computer icon shows you which servers or workstations you can reach in your own workgroup.

A network can contain a large number of computers (workstations). So that users do not entirely lose the overall picture, computers are allocated to workgroups (e.g. Sales, Marketing, Purchasing etc.) or **servers** and are also displayed in these categories.

Each station (server or workgroup) has a unique name which is required for accessing a particular computer. In the window above, you see for example both the *Pentium* and *London* workstations of the current workgroup in a network of workgroups.

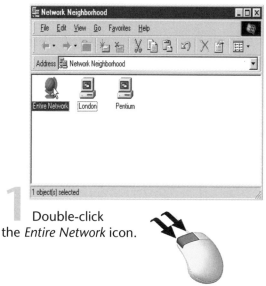

Double-click
the *Entire Network* icon.

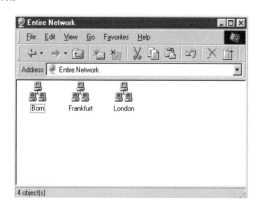

Windows opens the appropriate window and displays the servers and workgroups in the entire network.

This network only contains three workgroups with the names *Born, London* and *Frankfurt.*

305

2 Double-click the icon for the workgroup (in this case *Born*).

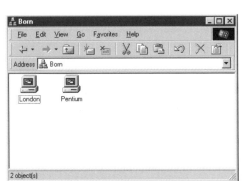

All the computers in the workgroup now appear (shown here is the *Born* workgroup with the *Pentium* and *London* workstations).

It might occur to you that this window contains the same computer names as the *Network Neighborhood* window. In a workgroup network you can interconnect computers into work groups (e.g. Sales, Marketing, Development etc.) and give them names. You will be assigned together with your computer as a workgroup user. Of course, assuming appropriate authorisation, you will also have the option of accessing computers in another workgroup via the *Network Neighborhood* icon. However, you will probably be working more frequently with printers and drives attached to the workstations of your own workgroup. Here it would be too laborious to choose the *Entire Network Neighborhood* icon every time and then the workgroup. To facilitate fast access to the computers of your own workgroup, Windows shows the individual stations directly in the *Network Neighborhood* window.

The following steps show you how to access the resources of a station within the workgroup. So return again to the *Network Neighborhood* window.

1 Click this button on the toolbar, or press the ← key.

Each time you do this it brings you to the folder at the next level up in the folder hierarchy (and to the folder displaying the workgroups).

2 Double-click a workstation icon.

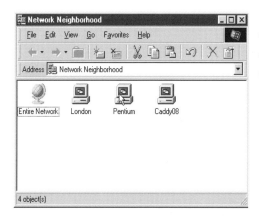

Here the *Pentium* workstation was chosen. (In your network, of course, the names will be different.)

Windows now displays the resources of the selected workstation in its folder window. However, the resources displayed are only those that have been **enabled** for sharing on the network by the user of that workstation. A **folder icon** stands for an enabled **folder** or **drive** on this workstation.

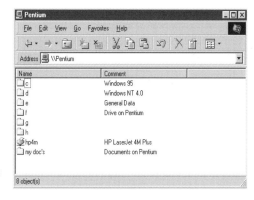

The printer icon means that the printer is attached to the computer whose folder is open and that the printer has been enabled for sharing within the workstation.

To work with a resource (a folder, for example), carry out the following steps:

1 Double-click a folder icon.

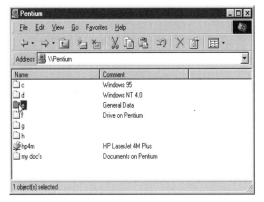

Here the folder *e* has been chosen.

The next few steps depend on whether or not a password request has been included for accessing the resource.

Here a password is
necessary.

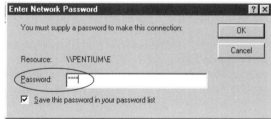

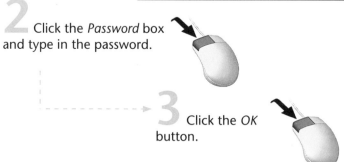

2 Click the *Password* box
and type in the password.

3 Click the *OK*
button.

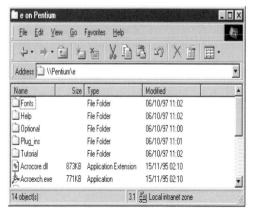

Windows now shows the
content of the chosen
resource (in this case the
content of the relevant drive *e*).
You can now work with the
files and subfolders of the
resource.

This works in the way shown in Chapter 3 in the example of the *My
Computer* window (only you don't see any drive icons). You can therefore
look at folders and files and delete, rename or copy them. You can also
load documents into programs.

309

It is entirely possible though that, when enabling sharing, the owner of a resource protects folders and files from modification by other users. General write-protection can be specified or a special **password** must be entered for **write-access** before changes can be made. If changes are not permitted, any attempt to move, rename or delete a file or folder will be refused by Windows, which will show the error message below.

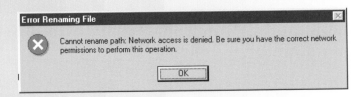

Pay attention when editing files with a program. If, for example, you load a letter from a write-protected (read-only) network resource, any changes you make to this document cannot be saved in the original file. Windows will refuse to save the document on that resource.

On no account must you use the *Network Neighborhood* icon on the desktop to get to a network resource. Either open the *Address* drop-down list box in the folder window or scroll through the Explorer bar in the Explorer window to find the *Network Neighborhood* icon and, if required, the icons of network resources currently being used.

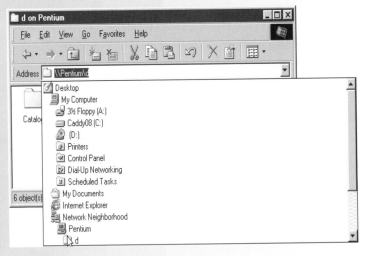

Mapping and disconnecting network drives

Would you rather work with drive icons in the Explorer window or in the *My Computer* window? Have you still got older programs that do not support access to network resources adequately or at all?

If so, you can assign (map) the name of a drive to a folder that has been enabled as sharable on the network. This drive is displayed in the *My Computer* folder. You can tell by the network cable icon that the drive is a network resource.

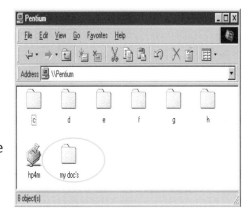

Are the *Map Drive* and *Disconnect* buttons missing from the toolbar of your folder window? In the Explorer window, you will find in the *Tools* menu the commands *Map Network Drive* and *Disconnect Network Drive*. You can also show the missing buttons in the toolbar by selecting the check box "Show Map Network Drive button in toolbar" on the View tab. To open this tab, choose the command *Folder Options* in the *View* menu of the Explorer or folder window.

To map such a drive to a folder (or other drive) enabled for shared use on another network workstation, only a few steps are necessary:

1 Open a folder window or Explorer window.

2 Click the *Map Drive* button in the toolbar.

3 In the *Drive* drop-down list box, change the drive letter for the sharable drive if this is necessary.

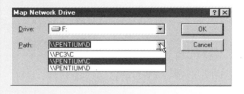

4 In the *Path* box, enter the path to the network resource.

The **path** to a **network resource** is generally entered in the form *Computername\Folder*. For example, the folder *Salary* on the computer *Pentium* would have the path*Pentium\Salary*.

Where a drive has already been allocated as a network resource, you can open the drop-down list box *Path* and click on the path you want.

If you select the check box "Reconnect at Logon", the next time Windows starts up it will automatically set up the mapping to the drive . The relevant computer must, however, be ready for operation.

To **remove** an **existing mapping** for a network drive, only two steps are necessary.

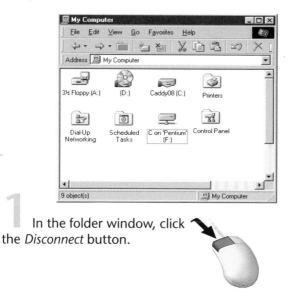

1 In the folder window, click the *Disconnect* button.

Windows opens the *Disconnect Network Drive* dialog box.

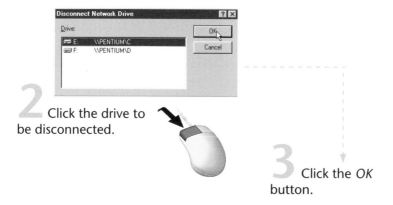

2 Click the drive to be disconnected.

3 Click the *OK* button.

Windows disconnects you from the network resource and removes the drive icon from the *My Computer* folder.

313

Printing on the network

Is your computer not attached to a printer? Do you want to use a particular printer for printing (e.g. a colour printer)? If your computer is in a network, you can use any network printer that has been enabled as sharable. Choosing a printer is as easy as using the local printer attached to your own computer.

1 In the application window, choose the FILE menu and click on the PRINT command. Alternatively, you can press the key combination Ctrl + P.

2 In the *Print* dialog box, click the *Name* drop-down list box.

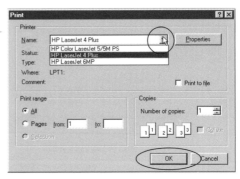

3 Choose the network printer you want to use.

4 Click the *OK* button to start the printout.

Setting up a network printer

To use a printer that has been enabled as sharable by another network station as if it were connected to your own computer, you first have to set it up. To do this proceed as follows:

1 Open the *Printers* folder (for example via the command SETTINGS / PRINTER in the Start menu).

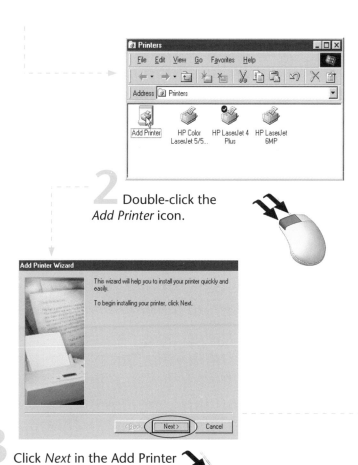

2 Double-click the *Add Printer* icon.

3 Click *Next* in the Add Printer Wizard window.

315

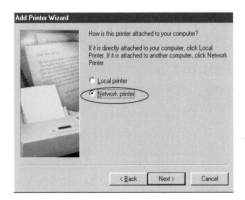

4 Activate the *Network Printer* radio button.

5 Click the *Next* button.

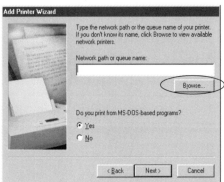

6 Click the *Yes* radio button if you want the printer to also use MS-DOS applications.

7 Enter the path for the printer or click the *Browse* button.

8 If you clicked *Browse*, search for the workstation printer and select it with the mouse.

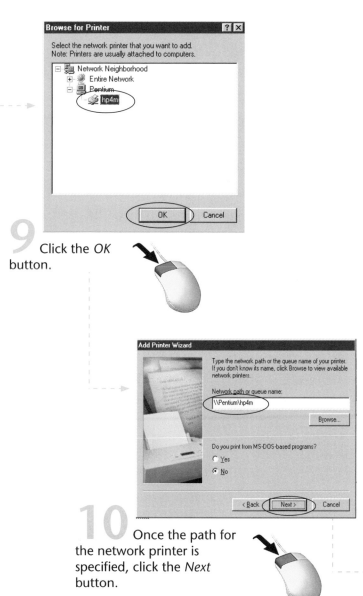

9 Click the *OK* button.

10 Once the path for the network printer is specified, click the *Next* button.

317

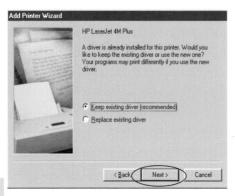

11 Choose whether Windows is to use a new or an existing printer driver.

12 Click *Next*.

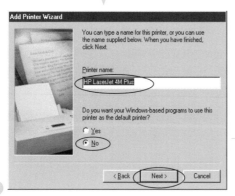

13 If necessary, change the printer name.

14 If necessary, specify the printer as the default printer for all Windows applications.

15 Click the *Next* button.

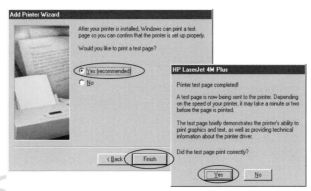

16 In the final step, choose whether you want Windows to print a test page, and click the *Finish* button.

Windows installs the printer and prints out the test page.

17 Confirm with the *Yes* button if the test page printout on the chosen network printer was correct.

The last few steps are generally similar to the procedure described in Chapter 6 for printer installation.

The network printer just set up is now displayed in the *Printer* folder as an icon. You can now use this printer like any other (local) printer.

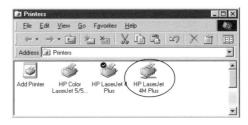

To set up the icon on the desktop, right-drag (i.e. drag with the right mouse button) the icon to the desktop and choose the command COPY SHORTCUT(S) HERE in the context menu. You can then very quickly open the window for this printer and control the print jobs in the queue of the network printer in question (see also Chapter 6).

Sharing printers

You can let other network users access the (local) printer connected to your PC. However, to do this, you must enable this printer for use as a shared resource.

1 Open the
Printers folder. - - - - - - → **2** Right-click with the mouse
on the icon of the printer you
want to share.

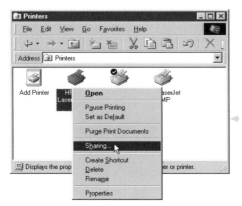

3 In the context menu, choose
the command *Sharing.*

Windows now opens the Properties window for the printer concerned.
Here we are only interested in the *Sharing* tab, which is already
displayed in the foreground. You now have to enter the sharing options
under this tab.

1 Click the *Shared
As* radio button.

2 Type in the Share Name (12 characters max.).

3 Also enter a comment to describe the printer.

4 If necessary, define a password and close the window via the *OK* button.

Windows will now enable the printer to be shared by other network users. Its printer icon will now appear in the *Printers* folder together with a small hand representing a shared resource.

TIP

The name you entered will be displayed for other users to see when they choose the computer in the Network Neighborhood window. On choosing the *Details* display, the user will also see your comment which gives further information on the type of printer. If you do not want every network user to be able to use the printer, enter a password in the appropriate box. When you close the sharing window, Windows allows you to confirm this password once more. On choosing this printer, another network user will be asked to enter the password; this must be entered correctly to obtain access to the printer.

CAUTION

If you have enabled your printer for sharing in the network, you will have to use it rather more carefully. You must not simply turn it off to cancel a print job, for example: it could in fact be another user's job. Also, when purging print jobs (see Chapter 6), you must take care and, if necessary, inform the other users on the network.

TIP

To disable sharing, activate the *Sharing* tab and select the *Not Shared* radio button.

Sharing drives and folders with other users

A complete drive or just a folder (together with its subfolders) can be made sharable on the network. To do this, only a few steps are necessary.

1 In the *My Computer* window or another window, right-click the drive or folder icon.

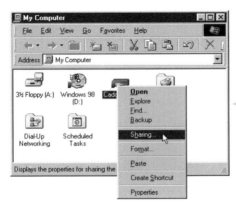

2 In the context menu, choose the command *Sharing*

Windows opens the window with the *Sharing* tab. You now have to specify the sharing options for the drive or folder.

3 Activate the *Shared As* radio button.

4 Enter the Share Name.

5 Define a comment for the shared resource.

6 Choose the type of access and, if necessary, allocate passwords for access to the resource.

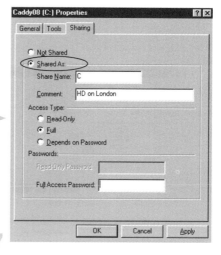

7 Close the tab via the *OK* button.

Windows now makes the drive available as a shared network resource with the options you have selected. You can recognise sharable drives by the hand that appears at the bottom left corner of the drive icon.

If you select the "Read-Only" access type, other users will only be able to read, and not modify, the data of the sharable resource. If users also have to modify the data, choose either "Full" or "Depends on Password". Depending on the option you choose, one or two passwords may then be specified. This enables you to allow read-only access to one user group, whilst a second password permits read/write access. If you leave the password boxes blank, every network user will be able to access the resource concerned as well as open and modify files or folders. Further information on the network functions is available in Windows Help.

323

What's in
this chapter?

When working with programs and files, data on the hard disk is frequently changed. This can cause errors which might lead to loss of data. To detect and remove errors and prevent data loss, this chapter shows you how to check disk drives using a program. In addition, you will learn how the hard disk can be edited by using a defragmentation program. This will allow Windows to read and save files faster. Furthermore, you will find out how to compress a drive and clean up a disk.

You already know about:

You are going to learn about:

Checking drives for errors

In Chapter 3 you were shown how to work with drives and diskettes. If you look back to that chapter, you will see that, when a diskette is formatted, a summary of the data on it is displayed. This summary also indicates the **number** of **defective sectors**, if there are any. These are areas of the diskette where no data can be stored.

A similar situation applies for other drives like hard disks. A hard disk can have damaged areas, a defective file allocation table (a kind of file index) and so on. The causes are many and diverse:

➡ The hard disk may be damaged in some places and data can no longer be stored there (this can occur, for example, if you push the computer quickly to another position when it is running, or accidentally knock it with your knee).

➡ Perhaps the computer has been turned off without previously shutting down Windows. This can also result from a power failure.

➡ Sometimes the program will no longer function (perhaps as the result of a system crash) and you can only get the computer to work again by turning it off and on again.

These and other factors result in **errors** on the **hard disk** or in the **file system** over time.

These and other errors lead over time to problems. You should therefore identify such errors and, if necessary, have them rectified using appropriate programs.

1 In the *My Computer* window, right-click the icon of the drive you want to check.

3 Activate the *Tools* tab.

2 In the context menu, choose the command PROPERTIES.

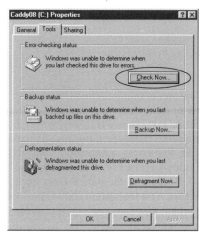

The *Tools* tab tells you the condition of the drive in terms of the last error check, the backup status and the last defragmentation.

4 Click the *Check Now* button.

327

Windows starts the *ScanDisk* program which displays the following window.

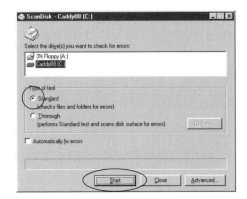

1 Select the drive you want to check for errors, if different from that displayed in the box.

2 Click the *Standard* type of test.

3 If required, specify further options.

4 Initiate the check by clicking *Start*.

Checking folders...

The course of the check is displayed in the progress window.

If ScanDisk finds errors on the drive, a window will appear with an appropriate message, as in the example shown here.

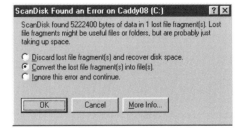

1 Now click a radio button option to specify the type of error correction.

2 Confirm your choice by clicking *OK*.

It is safest to **save** the **defective sectors** in files. You can find these files later in the main folder for the drive under names like *File0001.chk*, *File002.chk* etc. It may be possible to recover any lost text from these files. Otherwise, delete the files you don't need.

Occasionally, when the test program is activated, Windows reports that the disk is locked. In this case, close the window containing the drive from which the properties window was called up.

At the end of the check a summary of results for the disk is displayed.

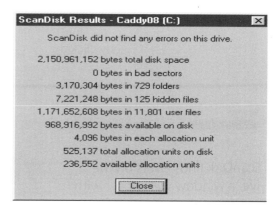

Whether the results summary appears and how the check is carried out can be set via the various options.

329

In the scanDisk window, if you choose the *Thorough* test option, a **surface scan** of the **disk** will also be carried out. In addition to defects in the file system, this check can also detect defective ares on the diskette/hard disk. If you choose the *Thorough* type of test, the following window can be opened via the *Options* button.

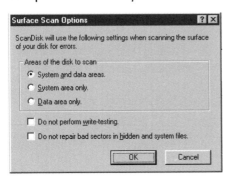

In this dialog box you can choose the areas of the disk for ScanDisk to check when scanning the surface.

In the ScanDisk window there is a button labelled *Advanced*, which you can use to activate a window containing additional options.

You should routinely check the disk drives on your computer for these kinds of errors. This prevents loss of data and indicates incipient problems with the hard disk or drive

Defragmenting drives

A diskette or hard disk is divided into separate blocks which are used by the file system for storing files. The file system always allocates free blocks for file data. Changing or deleting files leads to a file rarely using contiguous blocks: it's more likely that file data will be arbitrarily scattered among the blocks of the hard disk. This has the effect of making Windows slower and slower when reading and saving files (the individual blocks belonging to a file must first be found on the hard disk). However, there is a program which can be used to defragment files on a hard disk. This program relocates the file data so that it lies in contiguous blocks. To defragment a drive, proceed as follows:

1 Open a window displaying the drive.

2 Right-click the drive icon using the mouse.

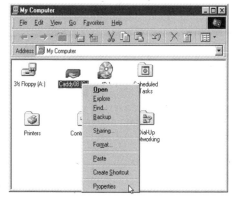

3 Choose the command PROPERTIES.

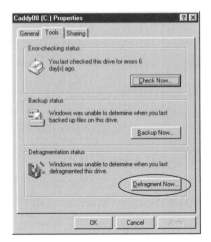

4 Under the *Tools* tab, choose the *Defragment Now* button.

The defragmentation program now checks to what extent the files are scattered over the blocks on the hard disk. This scattering is called **fragmentation**. If defragmentation is of benefit, the program will be started immediately.

You see the status of the defragmentation process in the *Disk Defragmenter* dialog box. You can pause by clicking the *Pause* button.

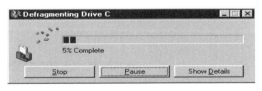

Clicking the *Show Details* button displays a window with a graphical representation of the fragmentation.

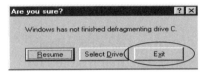

If you click the *Stop* button, the program asks you to confirm by showing the *Are you sure?* dialog box. Click *Exit* to exit the program.

The *Select Drive* dialog box appears as soon as you click the *Select Drive* button in the *Are you sure?* dialog box (or on activating the program via the Start menu).

Clicking the *Settings* button in the *Select Drive* dialog box opens the window opposite. In this dialog box, you can specify whether program files are to be rearranged and the disk checked for errors.

Compressing drives

A floppy disk (diskette) or hard disk has a certain capacity. Owing to the increasing size of many application programs, the storage capacity of the hard disk can soon be filled up. This means either deleting programs and files or installing a new larger hard disk. The ideal way, however, is to compress the files (or drive content). This operation involves a clever process of "packing" the data and then saving it. If you are faced with the same problem of a hard disk running out of space, here are two pieces of good news:

➡ Compression can fit between 50% and 200% more data on a drive. The amount of space you save depends on the data that is stored on the drive (text and many graphics can be compressed particularly well).

➡ Windows 98 has built-in functions to support drive compression. You can continue to use a compressed drive in the normal way – but you will fit more on it.

To compress a drive, proceed as follows:

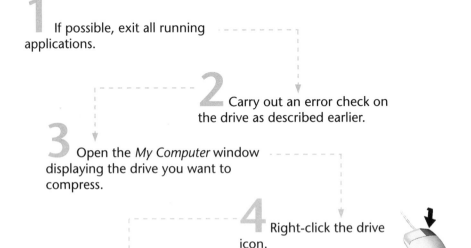

1 If possible, exit all running applications.

2 Carry out an error check on the drive as described earlier.

3 Open the *My Computer* window displaying the drive you want to compress.

4 Right-click the drive icon.

5 In the context menu, choose the command PROPERTIES.

The information under the *Compression* tab shows you how much storage space you can expect to gain by compressing.

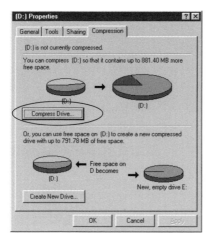

6 Click the *Compress Drive* button.

In a further dialog box, Windows shows the expected storage capacity.

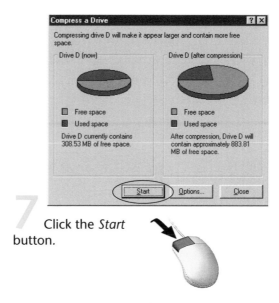

7 Click the *Start* button.

Windows then guides you through the steps for compression.

Compressing a drive can take several hours, during which time you cannot work on your PC. Compression packs the data into a compression file on the original drive. You must therefore never delete a file with a name like *Drvspace.001*, otherwise the compressed drive will be deleted and all the data on it lost!

The *Options* button in the *Compress a Drive* dialog box opens the *Compression Options* dialog box. In the *Free space on host drive* box, specify how much space you want to remain on the uncompressed drive. If you select the check box *Hide host drive*, the uncompressed drive will be hidden in the *My Computer* folder window.

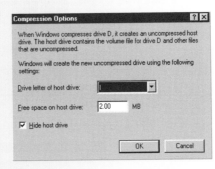

Cleaning up drives

If a drive is full, it can sometimes be helpful to clean up this drive and delete files that are no longer required. Windows has a built-in function called *Disk Cleanup* which can be used to clean up the drive. To use this function, proceed as follows:

1 Open the *My Computer* window displaying the drive.

2 Right-click the drive symbol.

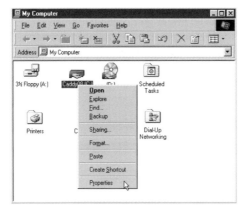

3 In the context menu, choose
the command PROPERTIES.

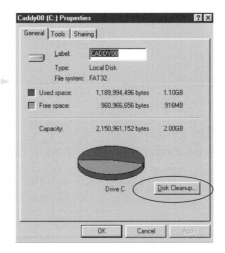

4 Under the *General* tab, click the
Disk Cleanup button.

Windows now checks the drive for files that can be deleted. Basically,
these include the contents of the Recycle Bin and temporary Internet
files.

The results of the check are displayed in a dialog box.

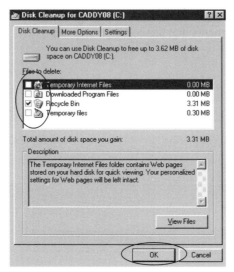

5 Select the check boxes for the files you wish to delete.

6 Click the OK button.

Windows starts the Disk Cleanup program and deletes the files concerned. Progress is displayed in a window as shown here.

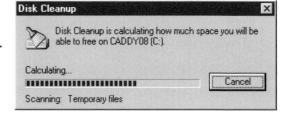

TIP

Where there is a shortage of space, Windows can run Disk Cleanup automatically. This option can be toggled in or out via the *Settings* tab. The *Further Options* tab allows experienced users to free up further storage space by removing Window components that are no longer needed.

Customising Windows

What's in this chapter?

Windows can be adjusted in many areas. Is the Windows clock wrong or do you want to set the date? This chapter shows how this can be corrected with a few mouse clicks. In addition, you will find out how to adjust the properties of the display and so activate background pictures and screen savers. Another topic covers the installation of programs and setting them up in the Start menu. You will learn how to add Windows components retrospectively and how to install programs on the computer. We also show how you can, for example, change the mouse settings.

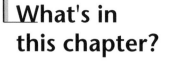

You already know about:

You are going to learn about:

Setting the date and time

In the bottom right corner of the screen Windows displays the time and, if activated, the date. You have already met these in Chapter 1. But what if the clock is telling the wrong time or the date is incorrect? This is no real problem: you only need a few mouse clicks to adjust the time or set the date.

1  Double-click the time in the bottom right corner of the taskbar.

Windows now opens the dialog box displaying the current time and the calendar, which includes the month and year.

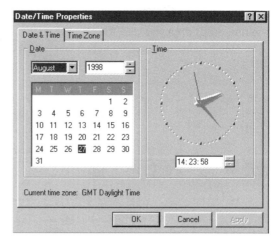

To adjust the time, proceed as follows:

1 In the time box, click the hours, minutes or seconds reading.

2 Enter the new value or change the setting by clicking the up and down buttons.

3 Click either *OK* or *Apply*.

The new time setting is displayed directly on the clock-face.

CAUTION

On activating the *Date & Time* tab, the clock still runs. You can tell this by the seconds hand stepping round. Once you change the value in the time settings box, the time stops until you click the *OK* or *Apply* buttons.

But if you want to reset the date, the following steps are required:

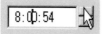

1 Select the year box and adjust the value if necessary. To do this you only need to click the up and down buttons.

2 If necessary, open the drop-down list box showing the months.

343

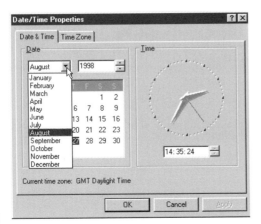

Click the month you want
to set.

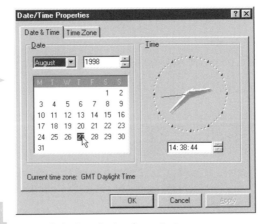

Now click the desired
day of the week.

The current day is marked by a coloured background.

5 Close the dialog box via the *OK* button.

Via the *Date & Time* tab, you can find out at any time on what day of the week a particular date falls (between 1980 and 2099). You only have to change the year and month. As soon as you change the year by means of the up and down buttons, the associated days change in the calendar box. If you close the tab by clicking *Cancel*, the current date remains unchanged.

The Date/Time Properties box has a second tab for setting the required **time zone**. This also determines, amongst other things, the form of display for the date and time. For the British Isles, the Greenwich Mean Time Zone is used. If you wish to change the time zone, proceed as follows:

1 Open the drop-down list box showing the time zones.

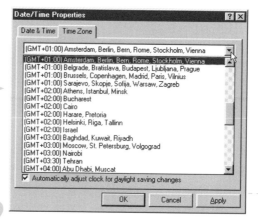

2 Choose the time zone you want.

345

3 Click the *Apply* button to activate the time zone.

Changing the desktop background

The Windows **desktop** background can be white (as in this book), coloured or patterned and, if you wish, even decorated with **wallpaper**. This gives you the option of customising the desktop. You could, for example, **scan in** a holiday photo and display it as the background on the screen.

To transfer images as files into a computer, you need a special device called a **scanner**. This works like a photocopier, but transmits the pattern to the computer. Once you have saved a page (e.g. a photo) as a *.bmp*-file, it can be displayed by Windows and used as wallpaper.

After installation, Windows will probably display a dark-green background on your screen for the desktop . In this book, however, a white background has been used to make the icons easier to see. If you want to change the colour of the desktop background, proceed as follows:

1 Right-click any free area of the desktop.

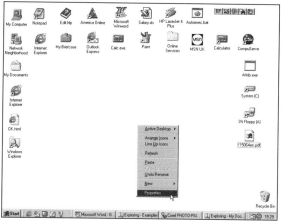

2 In the context-menu, right-click the command PROPERTIES.

3 Activate the *Appearance* tab.

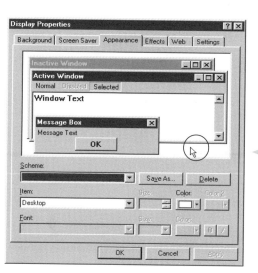

4 In the preview window showing how the window elements will look, click the area with the current background colour (arrowed).

347

The name *Desktop* should appear in the *Item* box. If not, choose this entry from the *Item* drop-down list, opened by clicking anywhere inside the box.

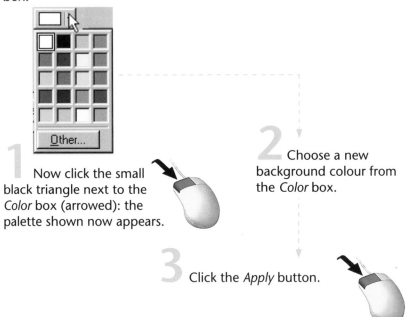

1 Now click the small black triangle next to the *Color* box (arrowed): the palette shown now appears.

2 Choose a new background colour from the *Color* box.

3 Click the *Apply* button.

Windows now colours in the desktop with the background colour you have chosen.

Under the *Appearance* tab, Windows offers you predefined, colour-matched settings for the desktop. You only have to open the *Scheme* list box and choose the relevant scheme. The preview then shows what the particular colour combination will look like.

Scheme:

Windows Standard
Rainy Day
Red, White, and Blue (VGA)
Rose
Rose (large)
Slate
Spruce
steve s.
Storm (VGA)
Teal (VGA)
Wheat
Windows Standard
Windows Standard (extra large)
Windows Standard (large)

Besides a solid coloured **background, patterns** and **pictures** can also be used on the desktop; choosing these is very easy. Background pictures only have to be saved with the file type *.bmp* in the Windows folder. To provide the desktop background with a pattern or picture, proceed as follows:

1 Right-click on any free area of the desktop.

2 In the context menu, choose the command PROPERTIES.

3 Activate the *Background* tab.

These steps correspond to the procedure described above for changing the background colour (only a different tab is used).

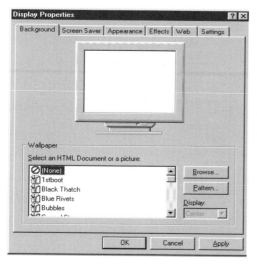

In the monitor graphic, the *Background* tab shows you a preview of the current pattern (called the "wallpaper") or background picture. You also see another list box for selecting the background.

349

To choose a pattern as background, proceed as follows:

1 Click the *Pattern* button.

Windows opens a dialog box for choosing the pattern.

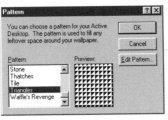

2 Click the item for the pattern you want.

3 Close the *Pattern* dialog box by clicking its *OK* button.

4 Close the *Background* tab via the *OK* button.

Here you see a desktop with a triangular pattern as background. The icon lettering is also given the background colour you set above.

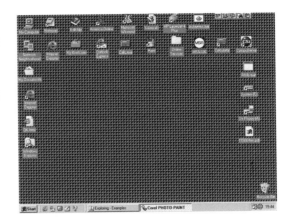

Alternatively, instead of a background pattern, you can **wallpaper** your **desktop** with a **picture** or an **HTML document**. There are some *.bmp*-files available in Windows that are useful for the wallpaper although you can choose others. If necessary, these can even be created or edited using the Windows Program *Paint*. To use a **picture** or an **HTML document** as the **desktop background**, proceed as follows:

1 Open the *Background* tab.

2 Choose the picture or HTML document you want from the *Wallpaper* list box and click its name.

3 If you like the wallpaper, click the *OK* or *Apply* button.

Windows will now display your picture or HTML document as the desktop background.

Maybe instead of a picture or HTML document you would like to put a Web page on the desktop as an *Active desktop* Element? This can be done using the following steps:

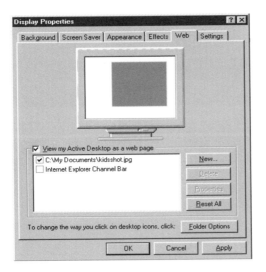

1 Activate the *Web* tab and make sure the "View my Active desktop as a Web page" check box is selected.

2 Click the *New* button.

Windows asks if you want to load a Web page from the Internet by visiting the Active desktop gallery on the Microsoft Web site. If you have a Web document on the local computer, close this dialog box by clicking *No*.

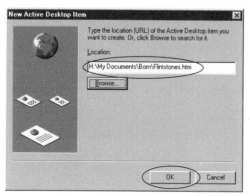

3 Enter the path for the HTML document in the *Location* box or choose the location by clicking *Browse*.

4 Close the dialog box by clicking *OK*.

5 Close the *Web* tab via the *OK* button.

Windows adds the Web page to the desktop as elements. If this page contains hyperlinks, the related documents can be opened by clicking them.

You can remove Web pages and save them as files using the Windows program FrontPage Express.

Setting up a screen saver

Windows offers a **screen saver** function. This is a program that detects if the computer has been inactive for a while (i.e. there has been no keyboard input or mouse movement). The program then switches from the desktop display to an animated screen pattern of your choice.

In the case of older monitors you sometimes see a burnt-in "pattern" when they are turned off. The purpose of the screen saver is to prevent a steady image (such as the desktop) being "burnt into" the monitor if it is displayed for long periods.

Depending on its type, the monitor can also be switched to the energy-saving mode after a certain waiting time.

To use one of the Windows screen savers, you first have to configure it. This is done in a similar way to changing the background picture:

1 Right-click on any free area of the desktop and choose the command PROPERTIES in the context menu.

2 Activate the *Screen Saver* tab.

Locate the screen saver options box.

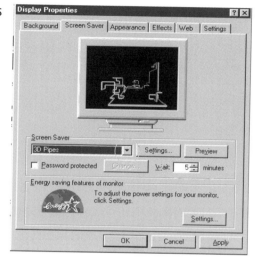

1 Open the *Screen Saver* drop-down box and click the item of your choice.

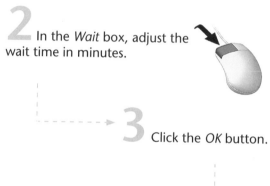

2 In the *Wait* box, adjust the wait time in minutes.

3 Click the *OK* button.

Windows now applies your settings for the screen saver. This becomes active after the system has been inactive for longer than the preset waiting time. As soon as you press a key or move the mouse, the desktop display reappears and you can continue working with your computer.

As soon as you choose the screen saver, the theme is displayed in the preview box on the *Screen Saver* tab. Click the *Preview* button to display the theme over the entire desktop. Just move the mouse to return to the tab. Depending on the screen saver you choose, you can specify various options by means of the *Settings* button.

If your monitor supports the energy-saving features, click the *Settings* button in the group "**Energy saving features of monitor**". Windows opens a second dialog box with tabs. Here you can set waiting times before these functions are activated (the monitor, hard disks turned off etc.).

The *Password protected* check box enables you to activate the **password request** for the **screen saver**. The password can be specified by means of the *Change* button. If this option is activated, you will need a password to return to the normal desktop when the screen saver is active. You should therefore either deactivate the password protection or use it with appropriate caution.

Changing the screen resolution

Windows allows the screen resolution to be selected. The higher the resolution, the more picture elements can fit onto the desktop. On the other hand, the desktop elements and windows reduce in size as resolution increases. After installing Windows, the screen is set to a default resolution of 640 x 480 pixels. However, depending on the size of the monitor and the installed graphics card, you can choose higher resolutions.

The screen content is represented by a pattern of coloured dots (also called pixels) arranged in lines. The number of coloured dots per row and the number of picture lines is known as the (screen) **resolution**. Each dot on the screen can be assigned a particular colour. The number of different colours that are used on the screen can also be adjusted and is sometimes called the **colour palette**.

To do this, proceed as follows:

1 Right-click on any free area of the desktop and choose the command PROPERTIES in the context menu.

2 In the *Display Properties* dialog box, activate the *Settings* tab.

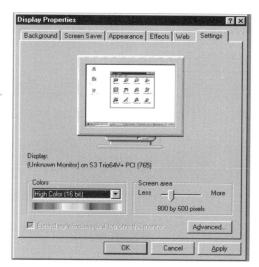

3 Drag the "Screen area" slider in the direction "Less" or "More".

4 Click the *Apply* button.

In Step 3 only those resolutions actually supported by the computer graphics card can be chosen. To change the resolution, Windows has to switch over the display.

A number of dialog boxes are therefore displayed before and during the changeover. Choose the appropriate buttons in the dialog boxes.

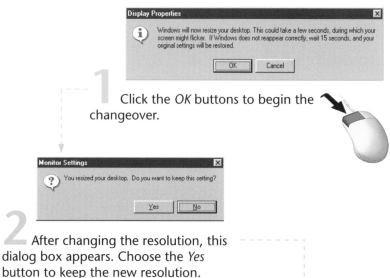

Click the *OK* buttons to begin the changeover.

After changing the resolution, this dialog box appears. Choose the *Yes* button to keep the new resolution.

If the desktop is not displayed correctly at the new resolution, choose the *No* button.

If the screen remains dark after changing over, or you cannot make out anything, you only need to wait about 15 seconds. Windows will then switch back automatically to the old resolution.

If the changeover has been successful, you should check if the resolution you have chosen is in fact practical. Even at moderately high resolutions, icons and text on smaller monitors can be very difficult to read. In this case, it is preferable to use a reduced resolution of 640 x 480 or possibly 800 x 600 pixels.

Installing Windows components

Windows is installed with certain programs and functions as standard (mostly by the computer manufacturer). Maybe some of the functions are missing from your system (e.g. games, desktop wallpapers, screen savers etc.)? Provided you have the Windows CD-ROM, you can very easily add these missing programs later on.

1 Insert the Windows CD-ROM in the drive.

2 When the Windows "Welcome window" opens, you can close it again immediately.

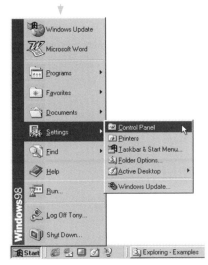

3 In the Start menu, click the command SETTINGS / CONTROL PANEL.

4 In the *Control Panel* window, double-click on the *Add/Remove Programs* icon.

5 Activate the *Windows-Setup* tab.

After a short time, Windows displays the individual component groups on this tab that you can add or remove retrospectively. If a check box on a particular line is selected, then at least one component of the group is installed.

To choose the components in a group, proceed as follows:

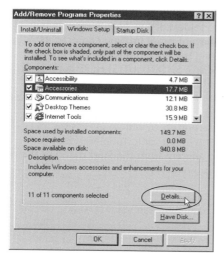

2 Click the *Details* button.

1 On the *Windows Setup* tab, select the check boxes for the various components you want to add.

3 In the list that appears, select the check boxes for the components that you want to install.

If the entry consists of several individual components, you can click *Details* to open a further dialog box and select the components.

361

4 Now close the dialog boxes by clicking their respective *OK* boxes.

5 *Click Apply* on the *Windows Setup* tab.

Windows now carries out the changes required for the configuration.

Windows checks all the component changes you have made in the component menu. Components associated with previously selected options that have now been cleared will be removed. In the case of newly selected components, Windows will install the necessary files from the CD-ROM. Clearing a selected component will remove the related functions. For many components, you will need to restart your computer before the changes become effective. A dialog box will inform you if a restart is necessary. You can either initiate the restart directly via the *Yes* button or execute it later by choosing *No*.

Installing programs

To use a new Windows program, in most cases you will have to install it from a CD-ROM or diskette. To do this, only a few steps are necessary.

1 Insert the CD-ROM or diskette into the appropriate drive.

2 Open the *My Computer* window and double-click the drive icon.

3 Look for the installation program in the drive window.

4 Start the program by double-clicking its icon.

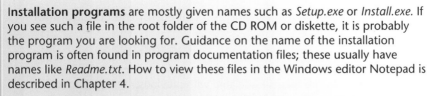

5 Follow the instructions for the installation program.

The window opposite shows the content of the Microsoft Office 97 CD-ROM together with the relevant installation program.

In the case of many CD-ROMs, a window opens automatically after insertion. Installation programs can often be chosen by clicking buttons in this window.

Changing the Start menu

When installing programs, an icon is also usually entered in the Start menu. Often the situation arises where entries have to be changed in the Start menu. Either entries which are no longer needed have to be removed, or there are cases where you want to include a program retrospectively in an existing or new group in the Start menu. To **remove** a **folder** (or a group) or a **program item** from the **Start menu**, the following steps are required:

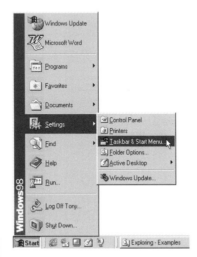

1 In the Start menu, click the command SETTINGS/ TASKBAR & START MENU...

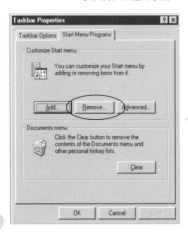

2 In the tab *Start Menu Programs* click the *Remove* button.

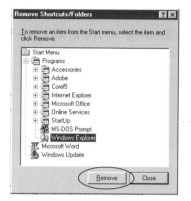

3 In the *Remove Shortcuts/Folders* dialog box, select the item you want to clear.

4 Click the *Remove* button.

As the Start menu is ultimately a (special) folder, you can treat this like the folder hierarchy of the Explorer bar. You open program group folders by double-clicking on the associated icon.

To **add** a **program** to the **Start menu**, carry out the following steps:

1 In the Start menu, choose the commands SETTINGS / TASKBAR & START MENU....

2 In the tab *Start Menu Programs*, click the *Add* button.

Windows now starts a Wizard that guides you through the remaining steps for setting up the program in the Start menu. In the following example, the Windows editor (Notepad) is entered directly into the PROGRAMS / ACCESSORIES menu.

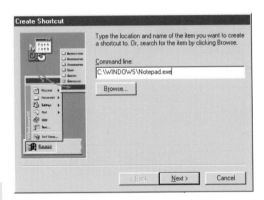

In the *Create Shortcut* dialog box shown, type in the command to call up the program. If necessary, use the *Browse* button to search for the folder containing the program.

Click *Next*.

Choose the folder in the Start menu where you want to place the program item. You can create a new folder using the *New Folder* button.

4 Click *Next*.

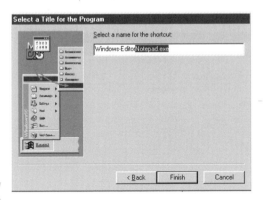

5 Enter the name that you want to appear in the Start Menu as the command.

6 Click the *Finish* button.

7 Close any windows still open.

If you now open the Start menu, you will see in the menu PROGRAMS / ACCESSORIES the (new) item for NOTEPAD, the Windows editor.

In this way you can add any program you like to the Start menu.

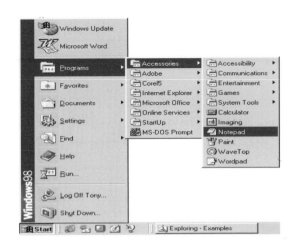

367

Did you find the above method too laborious? Then click the *Advanced* button on the *Start Menu Programs* tab. Windows then opens the window displaying the *Start menu* folder. As for other folders, you can work in this window and add or delete programs and folders. If you open a second window displaying the folder with the relevant program, you can drag its icon to the *Start menu* folder whilst holding the right mouse button down. You then set up the new item via the CREATE SHORTCUT(S) HERE command in the context menu. In addition, in Windows 98, you can drag a program icon using the mouse to the *Start* button. If you keep the left mouse button held down, the Start menu opens and you can move the icon to the desired position. When you release the left mouse button, Windows inserts the program icon at the current position in the menu. Unfortunately, however, you cannot rename the item. If you drag an item from the Start menu to the Recycle Bin, Windows will remove it from the menu.

Setting up a program icon on the desktop

A **shortcut** is a special technique that Windows uses to link an icon and name with a program or document file. You can, for example, create a shortcut on the desktop. All you need to do then is double-click on the icon to load the associated document or program.

You can set up a **program** you need to use frequently as a **shortcut** on the **desktop**. The program can then be started by double-clicking the icon.

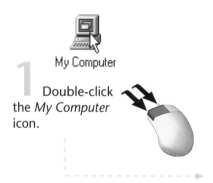

My Computer

1 Double-click the *My Computer* icon.

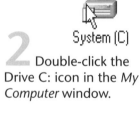

System (C)

2 Double-click the Drive C: icon in the *My Computer* window.

Windows

Notepad

3 In the Drive *C:* window, choose the *Windows* folder by double-clicking the folder icon.

4 Find the icon for the *Notepad.exe*. program in the *Windows* window.

5 Holding down the **right** mouse button, drag the *Notepad.exe* icon from the *Windows* window to the desktop.

6 As soon as the icon is outside the window in the desktop area, release the right mouse button.

7 In the **context menu**, click the command CREATE SHORTCUT(S) HERE.

Shortcut to
Notepad.exe

Windows now sets up the icon as a **shortcut** on the desktop. To start the *Notepad* program all you have to do is double-click its icon.

Using the method described above, you can create any shortcuts you want on the desktop. Chapter 3 shows how this is done for files and folders. In that chapter you can also see how to **rename** shortcuts. To **remove** a shortcut, drag its icon to the Recycle Bin.

Setting up DOS programs

Maybe you still have a couple of favourite DOS programs that you would also like to use with Windows 98? This is especially often the case with games. Like Windows programs, DOS programs can be started by double-clicking an icon for a *.exe*, *.com* or *.bat* file. You can create the icons as shortcuts on the desktop or enter them as items in the Start menu.

However, unlike Windows programs, all DOS programs are executed in a **DOS window.** You can set up the way you want Windows to handle the DOS window.

The most important settings are dealt with below for the example of the DOS program *Edit.com*. You will find this program in the Windows subfolder *Command*. To change the settings for the DOS program window, proceed as follows:

1 Open the folder window in which the DOS program is saved (in this case it is the Windows subfolder *Command*).

2 Right-click the DOS program icon and choose the command PROPERTIES in the context menu.

3 Enter the DOS program options on the individual tabs.

4 Close the window by clicking *OK*.

Next time you start the program, Windows applies the defaults you set for the DOS program. On the various tabs, for instance, you can choose whether you want the DOS program to run in a window or to use the whole screen.

Many DOS programs, though, do not run under Windows. In Windows 98 you can ensure that when a DOS program starts, its own DOS version is automatically loaded.

1 Click the *Advanced* button on the *Programs* tab (see above).

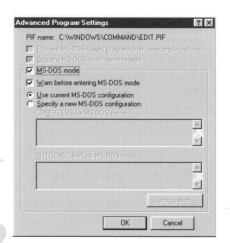

2 In the *Advanced Program Settings* dialog box that then opens, select the "MS-DOS Mode" check box.

3 Close any open dialog boxes by clicking their *OK* buttons.

If you now start the DOS program, Windows shuts down and DOS is loaded. After the DOS program is exited, the computer reloads Windows into the memory.

Many DOS programs use special memory areas with names like **EMS** and **XMS** etc. These memory options can be set up on the *Memory* tab according to the manufacturer's specification. When *Auto* is set, the program can request the necessary memory itself.

> With the setting *No*, a particular memory area is switched off. It is beyond the scope of this book to go into the detailed memory setting requirements of DOS programs. The manufacturer's program documentation normally contains guidance on how to choose the settings for Windows.

> Guidance on the other tab options can be found in Windows Help. Right-click the element you need help on and then left-click the *What's This?* button that appears. Windows then opens a window giving additional information.

373

Configuring the mouse

Are you left-handed or doesn't double-clicking with the mouse work particularly well? Then you should adjust the mouse settings to your requirements.

1 In the Start menu, choose the command SETTINGS / CONTROL PANEL.

2 Mouse
In the *Control Panel* window, double-click the mouse icon.

Windows now opens the tabbed Mouse Properties dialog box.

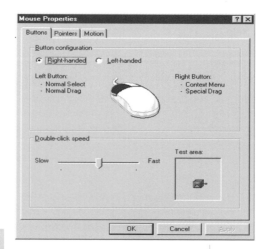

1 If you are left-handed, click the *Left-handed* radio button on the *Buttons* tab.

2 To change the speed of double-clicking, drag the "Double-click speed" slider to the right or left.

3 To test, double-click in the test area. If the head of a jack-in-the box appears, the double-click is working.

Once you close the Properties dialog box by clicking the *OK* button, Windows applies the new settings.

Other icons in the Control Panel can be used to set additional Windows options. For further information, please refer to Windows Help.

Computer startup problems

Nothing happens after switching on

Check the following points:

→ Are all plug and socket connections properly made?

→ Is the monitor turned on?

→ Is power available at the socket?

The computer reports: Keyboard Error or no keyboard present, Press F1 to continue

Check the following points:

→ Is the keyboard connected?

→ Is something resting on the keyboard?

→ Perhaps one of the keys is stuck?

Now press the Function key F1.

The computer reports: Non-system disk or disk error

There is probably a diskette in floppy disk drive A. Remove the diskette and restart the computer.

Keyboard and mouse problems

After startup, the numeric keypad keys do not work correctly

On the right-hand side of the keyboard is a key block (called the numeric keypad), which you can use to enter numbers. If numbers cannot be entered with these keys, press the Num key. This key is also called the NumLock key and is located in the top left corner of the numeric keypad. As soon as the *Num* indication lights up on the keyboard, you can type in numbers. Pressing the Num key again switches the keyboard back and you can use the cursor keys of the keypad.

Several characters appear at once when pressing a key

The keyboard has a repeat function. If you press a key for a slightly longer time, the computer repeats the character. Maybe you are pressing the key for too long. You can adjust the time before which the Windows repeat function is activated.

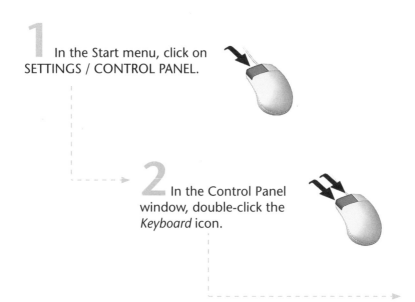

1 In the Start menu, click on SETTINGS / CONTROL PANEL.

2 In the Control Panel window, double-click the *Keyboard* icon.

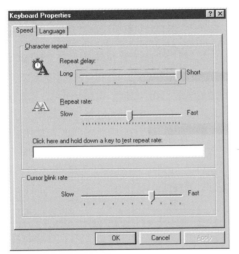

3 Activate the *Speed* tab.

4 Change the settings for *Repeat rate* and *Repeat delay*.

You can check the settings in the test area and then close the window by clicking *OK*. If this does not rectify the problem, check whether a key may have stuck or the keyboard is damaged (the switch for the key "bounces": each time it is pressed, it outputs several characters).

Some keys produce the wrong characters

This will happen if the keyboard is set up for another language so that the UK English **keyboard driver** is not installed (this is the program for controlling the keyboard).

1 In the Start menu, click on SETTINGS / CONTROL PANEL.

2 In the Control Panel window, double-click the *Keyboard* icon.

3 Activate the *Language* tab.

The keyboard must be set to *English (British)* or whatever language you wish to work in.

If several languages are available, choose *English (British)* and close the window. If this is missing, you will have to install it again by clicking the *Add* button. Windows guides you through the steps required.

The mouse pointer does not move at all or not correctly

Check the following points:

➡ Is the mouse properly connected to the computer?

➡ Is the mouse being used on a mouse mat?

➡ Perhaps the mouse ball is dirty?

After extensive use of the mouse, the part that detects mouse movements gets dirty. Remove the ball on the underside of the mouse. You will see some little wheels. If these are dirty, clean them using a cotton bud. Also you shouldn't place the mouse on a smooth surface as otherwise the ball will not roll properly.

379

The mouse buttons are interchanged or double-clicking does not work

The following fault pattern occurs: Left-clicking brings up the context menu, whereas right-clicking selects something. This means the effect of the left and right buttons is interchanged. Cause: You have a mouse for left-handers. Remedy: Learn how to operate left-handed, or ...

1 ... In the Start menu, click SETTINGS / CONTROL PANEL.

2 Double-click the *Mouse* icon in the Control Panel window.

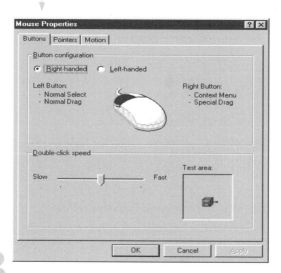

3 Activate the *Buttons* tab and set the *Button configuration* to *Right-handed.*

As soon as the window closes, the mouse buttons should again work correctly. Do you have **problems** with **double-clicking?** On this tab you can also change double-click speed for improved mouse operation.

Do you work with a laptop? Then activate the *Motion* tab and select the check box "Show pointer trails". In addition, on this tab you can also set how fast the mouse pointer moves.

Windows desktop problems

The text "Protected Mode" appears on the desktop

On startup Windows detected a problem and started the computer in protected mode. This occurs if Windows has not been shut down properly. Exit Windows and try to restart the computer. In most cases everything now proceeds normally.

Icons cannot be moved on the desktop

If desktop icons automatically jump back to their old position after you have moved them with the mouse, carry out the following steps:

1 Right-click on any free area on the desktop.

2 In the context menu, choose the command ARRANGE ICONS.

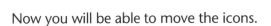

3 In the submenu, cancel the selection of the command AUTOMATICALLY ARRANGE by means of a single click.

Now you will be able to move the icons.

A shortcut was deleted by mistake

If you have deleted a shortcut by mistake, you can open the context menu immediately afterwards by right-clicking with the mouse and choosing the command UNDO DELETE. Otherwise you will have to create the shortcut again (see Chapter 11).

A program is missing from the Start menu

You will have to enter the program in the Start menu yourself. The way to do this is shown in Chapter 11.

A program cannot be found on Startup

On starting a program via a shortcut or the Start menu, the window opposite 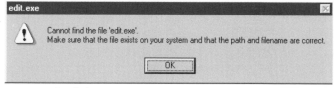 appears. Windows cannot find the program.

You have deleted the program file or moved it to another folder. If the program is still on the hard disk, modify the path to this program in the Shortcut Properties window.

The taskbar is missing, has been moved or is too large

The taskbar can be moved on the desktop by means of the mouse to any side of the screen. It can also be moved to the margin where it will only be seen as a grey bar. Use the mouse to drag the taskbar to the position you want. Sometimes the taskbar will disappear as soon as a window is maximised. You can adjust these taskbar settings in the start menu via the commands SETTINGS / TASKBAR & STARTMENU. On the *Taskbar Options* tab, select the check box "Always on top".

The clock is not displayed in the Taskbar

1 In the Start menu, click on
SETTINGS / TASKBAR & STARTMENU.

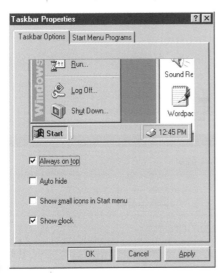

2 On the *Taskbar Options* tab, select
the check box "Show clock".

3 Close the window.

Pattern or wallpaper appears or is hidden

If you want to change the setting for the desktop-background (show/
hide wallpaper or pattern), this is done via the Display Properties window.
The procedure is explained in Chapter 11.

The screen saver does not work

The screen saver will only be activated if the computer has been inactive
for a certain time. If an application window is open, the screen saver does
not always appear. If necessary, also check the settings on the *Screen
Saver* tab (see Chapter 11).

383

Forgotten your screen saver password?

Did you set up the screen saver with a password? Is the screen saver active and you can't remember the password?

Now that's awkward! From now on follow the recommendation in Chapter 11 and dispense with password protection for the screen saver. If you do slip up, carry out the following steps:

1 Switch off the computer (if you were editing a file in a program and didn't save it, you will have lost the changes – there has to be a penalty somewhere!).

2 Start up the computer again and log in under Windows.

3 Open the Display Properties window and disable password protection for the screen saver (or define a new password).

How to set up the screen saver is described in Chapter 11.

Forgotten your Windows password?

Do you have to log in to Windows with a password? And you've forgotten it? Then bypass the login by pressing the ⌷Esc⌷ key. Launch Windows Explorer and look in the Windows folder for files with the extension *.pwl* (use the search pattern **.pwl*). Explorer will display a file with your name and the extension *.pwl*. Delete this file, shut down Windows and restart the computer. Now enter your name in the login window. When Windows asks for your password, enter a new one.

If you are networking, you should be given a new password by the network administrator. The trick shown does not work for Windows NT. Your administrator will have to assign you a new password.

Not all folders and files are visible in the window

Sometimes a window is too small. You can then use the scroll bars to scroll in the window and display the folders/files you want to see.

On choosing the channel bar, Internet Explorer appears in full-screen mode

Press function key F11 and Windows will switch Internet Explorer to window mode; press this key again to return to full-screen mode.

The toolbar is missing in the folder or Explorer window

With many programs you can show/hide the tool and status bars via the VIEW menu.

A program stops responding

Sometimes a program hangs: it stops responding to key input and mouse clicks.

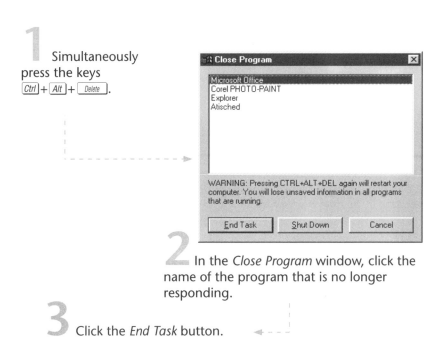

1 Simultaneously press the keys [Ctrl] + [Alt] + [Delete].

2 In the *Close Program* window, click the name of the program that is no longer responding.

3 Click the *End Task* button.

Windows now attempts to forcibly exit the program. If this cannot be done, a further window appears with the message that the program is not responding. You then have to choose the button to end the program.

Folders and files

File extensions do not appear

Are the extensions for some filenames missing from folder windows or Explorer?

In the VIEW menu, choose the command FOLDER OPTIONS.

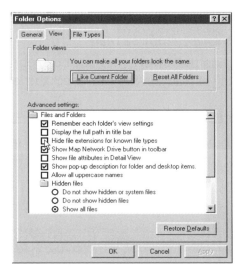

On the *View* tab, delete the check box selection "Hide file extensions for known file types".

Close the window.

Some files are not displayed

You are sure that a particular file is in a folder, but it appears neither in the folder window nor in Explorer? Choose VIEW / FOLDER OPTIONS; then activate the *View* tab. In the group "Hidden files" you must now select the radio button "Show all files". After closing the tab, you will see the hidden files. If need be, you will have to press the 🖂 key to update the view of the window.

Each folder is displayed in its own window

For every folder icon chosen in a folder window by double-clicking, Windows immediately opens another window. Choose VIEW / FOLDER OPTIONS; then select the radio button "Custom, based on settings you choose" on the *General* tab and click the *Settings* button. In the *Custom Settings* dialog box, select the radio button "Open each folder in the same window".

A diskette or CD ROM cannot be read

When double-clicking the drive, a message box appears informing you that the drive is not yet ready. In this case check the following points:

➡ Is the diskette or CD-ROM inserted in the drive?

➡ In the case of a CD-ROM, open and close the drive and wait a few seconds. Windows will then usually detect this as a change of CD.

➡ Has the diskette also been inserted in the drive right side up? If necessary, refer to Chapter 3 on how to insert a diskette into the drive.

➡ If the diskette you are using is new, this may not have been formatted, in which case you will have to format it before use (see Chapter 3).

Remove any error you find.

C:\My Documents

A:\ is not accessible.

The device is not ready.

Retry   Cancel

Click the
Retry button.

Sometimes it is necessary to click *Retry* several times. Alternatively, you can click the *Cancel* button and repeat the whole attempt again.

Failure of diskette save operation

On attempting to
save a file to a
diskette, a window
appears showing
this error message.

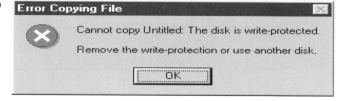

Error Copying File

Cannot copy Untitled: The disk is write-protected.

Remove the write-protection or use another disk.

OK

Remove the diskette from the drive and deactivate the write protection (see Chapter 3).

Failure of file update operation

You have loaded a document file in a program, updated the content and chosen the *Save* function. However, the program opens the *Save As* dialog box and suggests a new filename. If you enter the name of the old file, the program reports that the file is read-only (i.e. write-protected). In the case of CD-ROM files, this is obvious since you cannot change the content of a CD-ROM.

When CD-ROM files are copied, they become write-protected, although this write-protection can be removed.

1 Right-click the file icon.

2 In the context-menu, click the command PROPERTIES.

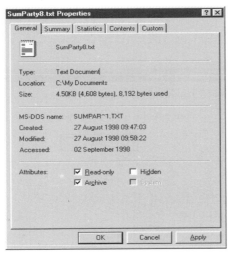

3 Remove the check mark from the "Read-only" check box.

4 Close the dialog box.

Printing problems

Printer not working

During printing the message shown opposite might appear. There is a printer error. Remove the error and choose the *Retry*. button.

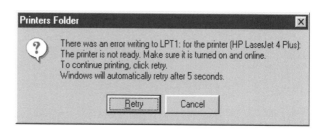

You can also cancel the printout by clicking the *Cancel* button. To rectify the printer error, you should check the following points:

➡ Is the printer turned on with power available?

➡ Is the printer cable between computer and printer connected correctly?

➡ Is the printer **online**?

➡ Has the printer enough paper, toner, or ink?

➡ Is there a fault on the printer (e.g. paper jam)?

➡ In the case of a network printer, have you perhaps chosen the wrong printer?

➡ Is the printer driver correctly set up (e.g. where there is a choice of printer connection)?

Removing landscape orientation

The printed output runs across the page. In this case, change the printer options from landscape to portrait orientation. Chapter 6 describes how to do this.

Printer draws paper from the wrong tray (Letter, A4),

Change the printer options for the paper source. Chapter 6 describes how to do this.

Graphics printout is too coarse

Sometimes graphics appear quite coarse during printing.

1 In the *Printers* folder, right-click the printer icon.

2 In the context menu, choose the command PROPERTIES.

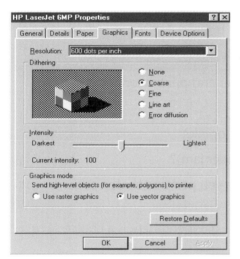

Print options for many printer's can be set in the printer's Properties window. For example, *Dithering* can be set to *Fine* in the *Graphics* tab.

Change the entry in the *Resolution* drop-down list box. *Print quality* may also be set on the *Device Options* tab.

A blank page is output for every printout

When printing, Windows can produce separator pages. If these are not needed, turn off the output in the Properties window for the printer in question.

Separator page: [none]   ▼   Browse...

1 Set the *Separator Page* option on the *General* tab to *(None)*.

With this option set, there should no longer be blank pages at the end of the printout.

Glossary

A

Access   Microsoft Access 97 is the name of a Windows **database**.

Account   Authorisation to log in to a computer via a data link and, for example, surf the WWW.

Address   Storage location in the address area (of main memory) of a computer; or the specification of the location of a Web page or the recipient of an e-mail message.

ANSI characters   ANSI is the abbreviation for American National Standards Institute and ANSI characters define the characters used under Windows.

AOL   Short name for America Online, a company that provides access to online services.

Application programs   that you can work with on a computer (e.g. Word, Excel, Access, Corel Draw etc.).

Arithmetic coprocessor
A special computing chip for mathematical computing calculations.

ASCII characters   ASCII is the abbreviation for American Standard Code for Information Interchange. The ASCII character set defines 127 characters (letters, numbers and special characters).

AUTOEXEC.BAT   A special file used by Windows for transferring settings on computer startup.

B

Backslash   The \ character (used for separating folder names).

Backup   The term used when making a duplicate copy of data (files are saved on diskette/tape).

Basic   Abbreviation for Beginners All-purpose Symbolic Instruction Code. Basic is a simple programming language that is easy to learn.

Baud   A measure of data-transmission speed over a serial interface.

Bit   The smallest unit of information in a computer (can take the values 0 or 1). 8 bits make 1 byte.

Bitmap   A format for storing pictures or graphics. Like on a screen, the image is divided into individual dots that are stored in rows.

Boot   To start a computer.

Browser   A program which can be used to display Web pages.

Bug   A software error in a program.

Byte   A byte is the unit of information consisting of 8 bits. A byte enables the representation of numbers from 0 to 255.

C

C   The name of a programming language.

Character set   The character codes available on the computer (ASCII, ANSI).

Chat   The name given to an Internet service in which participants can converse in so-called "chat rooms".

Chip   General term for an electronic component.

CIS   Abbreviation for CompuServe Information Service and the short name of the firm CompuServe which provides access to online services.

393

COM   Name for PC serial interfaces (e.g. COM1:).

Command   An instruction to a computer.

CONFIG.SYS   A special file that is used when starting up Windows.

CPU   Abbreviation for Central Processing Unit, the computational unit of a computer.

Cursor   An on-screen position indicator (icons: arrow, hand, vertical line, hourglass etc.).

D

Database   A program for storing, managing and querying data.

Desktop Publishing (DTP)   Preparing documents (brochures, books etc.) on a computer.

Dialog box   A window in which Windows requests a response from the user.

Download   Transfer data by **modem** to your computer from the Internet or other sources.

E

Editor   A program for creating and editing simple text files.

Electronic mail (e-mail) Messages sent by electronic means (see Chapter 8).

EMS   Abbreviation for Expanded Memory Specification, the name of a special memory technique.

Error   An error in a program.

Ethernet   A technique for transmitting data in networks.

Excel   The name of a Microsoft spreadsheet program.

F

FAT   Abbreviation for file allocation table. It is the method used by Windows for storing files on a diskette or hard disk.

File   Data is saved in files on floppy disks (diskettes) or hard disks (see Chapter 3).

Floppy disk   An older name for a diskette.

Font   The name given to all the characters in a typeface (Arial, Times Roman, Courier etc.)

Font size   Size of the letters, specified in points (pt).

Freeware   Software that is free to use and may only be distributed free of charge.

FTP   Stands for File Transfer Protocol. This function is used in the Internet for transmitting files between computers.

G

GB   Abbreviation for gigabyte (equal to 1000 megabytes).

GIF   A graphics format, used for graphics in Web pages.

Gopher   Name of a search service in the Internet.

Graphics card   A plug-in card in a PC for controlling the display.

H

Hardware   All the parts of a computer that can be physically touched (all devices).

High Memory Area (HMA) Part of the memory lying directly above the 1 MB boundary.

Home page   Start page of a person or company in the World Wide Web. Hyperlinks enable you to navigate from the home page to other Web pages.

HTML   Stands for Hypertext Markup Language, the document format on the Web.

Hyperlink   Reference in an HTML document to another Web page.

I

Internet   Worldwide connection of computers in a network (see Chapter 8).

J

Joystick   A device for controlling games programs.

JPEG   Graphics format used for graphics in Web pages.

K

Kbyte   Abbreviation for kilobyte (equal to 1024 bytes).

L

LAN   Abbreviation for Local Area Network, the name for a network within a company. (The opposite is a Wide Area Network).

LCD   Special display (Liquid Crystal Display) on laptop computers.

Lotus 1-2-3   A spreadsheet program from Lotus.

M

Mailbox   The name for an electronic form of letter box on a computer where you can collect messages addressed to you.

MB   Abbreviation for megabyte (1 million bytes).

Modem   Accessory used with a PC to transmit data over a telephone line; it is required for access to the Internet, for

395

example.

MS-DOS An older operating system from Microsoft.

Multimedia Techniques for integrating text, pictures, video and sound on the computer.

N

NetMeeting A Windows program for holding conferences on the Internet.

NetShow A Windows program for playing videos from the Internet.

Network Interconnection of computers for the exchange of data (see Chapter 9).

Newsgroups Discussion groups on specific topics on the Internet.

O

Online service A service for accessing the Internet; examples are T-Online, America Online and CompuServe.

Operating system A program (such as Windows) that takes control after the computer starts up.

Outlook Express A Windows program for creating, sending, reading and receiving e-mail.

Output device A device used to output documents you have created (e.g. screen, printer).

P

Packing density Diskettes (floppy disks) are available in two packing densities: **DD** (Double Density) and **HD** (High Density).

Parallel Interface A connection between a computer and a device (usually a printer).

Pascal A programming language that is often used on a PC.

Path Specifies the route from a hard disk to a file in a particular folder (e.g. c:\text\letters).

Processor Another name for the CPU.

Public Domain Software which is available to the public and may be freely copied and distributed with the permission of the author (compare freeware).

Q

QWERTY keyboard The name of the English keyboard (the first six keys on the second row make the word QWERTY).

R

RAM Abbreviation for Random

Access Memory; it is the name for the components which form the main memory of a computer.

Resolution   A measure specifying the number of dots that form a graphic (arranged as rows of dots, called pixels). Resolution determines the number of dots per line and the number of lines per picture (the same applies for screen resolution).

S

Scanner   Accessory for reading pictures or piece of text into the computer.

Screen saver   A program that prevents the image on the screen "burning into" the monitor when the computer is inactive.

Serial interface   The interface for a device connection (modem, mouse).

Server   The main computer on a network.

Shareware   Software that may be freely distributed and tried out. To use it regularly, the software must be registered with the program author for a small fee. This gives the user the opportunity to thoroughly test the software beforehand. The author can bypass expensive marketing and is therefore usually able to offer the software at a low price.

Software   Computer programs.

Spreadsheets   Programs for performing calculations very simply in tabular form.

U

Unix   An operating system which is particularly common in the world of large-scale computers (mainframes).

URL   Abbreviation for Uniform Resource Locator (address of a Web page).

User interface   The way in which the computer accepts information from the user and then displays it. Windows, for example, has a graphical user interface with icons and windows.

V

VGA   Graphics standard (16 colours and 640 x 480 dots or pixels). These days, Super-VGA is used with more colours and pixels.

Virus   A program that propagates and copies itself into other programs, frequently causing damage to programs, data or hardware. Usually, viruses infect the computer when a specific event occurs (e.g. on a particular day).

W

Web page   A document in HTML format.

Word processing   A program for creating letters, reports, books and so on (e.g. WordPad or Microsoft Word).

Working memory   The temporary storage (RAM) in a computer. Its size is specified in MB (megabytes).

WWW   World Wide Web, the part of the Internet which can be used to easily retrieve pages of text and pictures by means of a **browser**; usually referred to simply as the Web.

X

XMS   Abbreviation for Extended Memory Specification, the name for the extended memory of a PC above 1 MB.

Index

SYMBOLS

A

B

V

VGA graphics, definition 398
Video
– looking at 249
– setting window size 253
Virus 398

W

Wallpaper 346
Web page 266, 398
– bookmarks 283
– saving 286
Web server 265
Web style 30
Wildcard 123
Window
– closing 34
– full-screen size 33
– maximizing 33
– minimizing to icon 33
– moving 36
– opening 30
– opening icon 33
– resizing 34
– restoring to previous size 33
– switching 36
Windows
– background picture 187
– installing components 359
– password, forgetting 384
– shutting down 47
– Start menu 52
– starting 20
Word processing
– key combinations 140
WordPad 154
– document,
  loading 167
  saving 166
– first-line indent 165
– printing document 168

– setting indents 165
Wordwrap 157
Workgroup 304
Workgroup network 301
Working memory, definition 398
World Wide Web 264
WWW
– definition 398
– surfing 277

X

XMS, definition 398
XMS memory 373